C000039205

To Huxley George Bustillos McDonough

CONTENTS

ACKNOWLEDGEMENTS

We would like to thank Dr Stuart Isaacs, from University of West London, for his continuous advice and support on the publication of this work. We would also like to thank a number of scholars who gave up their time to read and critique our various chapters, including Dr Philippa Velija and Dr Dave Webber at Solent University, and Professor Norman Ginsburg and Dr James Morgan at London Metropolitan University. We would also like to thank Beatriz Corrales Dominguez for her research around UBI criticisms.

1

INTRODUCING A UNIVERSAL BASIC INCOME

Introduction

Imagine living in a society in which you are given money for nothing – a monthly cash sum with no strings attached. Imagine a world in which, by virtue of being a citizen, you're provided with enough cash to keep you over and above the poverty line. This might sound like a radical idea, or utopian, but is exactly the kind of world which is discussed and examined in this textbook – an idea which has been labelled (among other labels) a *universal basic income*. This idea is very controversial. For some, a universal basic income is a way forward, a way of achieving a more egalitarian world in which the lives of every citizen are looked after and cared for by the safety and economic security of the State. For others, a universal basic income is an extension of the 'nanny state'; an absurd idea, which is both unrealistic and unaffordable. It may stifle economic growth, crash the economy and even bankrupt the state. Whatever one's opinion, nobody can dismiss the fact that the idea of a universal basic income has been gathering a lot of attention, and is currently a 'hot topic' being discussed all over the globe. This popularity is not simply based on talk and debate, but is also based upon policy and practice, with countries such as Finland, Canada and India (among others) conducting 'basic income' pilots and experiments. What is your opinion about universal basic income? Is it a crazy idea which will never work or a sensible solution to solving society's social issues and social problems? You may already have an opinion and want to express it in academic writing or public debate. Or your thoughts may be emerging from the reading of this text. Whatever your stance, reading this textbook will provide 'food for thought', allowing you to extend your thinking and develop your arguments for or against a universal basic income. This textbook is primarily designed for undergraduate students wishing to learn about universal basic income, providing a reliable source which can be used for academic writing and discussion. It introduces the ideas of universal basic income by providing an overview of its principles, examples and current debates.

This chapter provides readers with an introduction to universal basic income by examining what it is and discussing it in relation to other welfare provisions. It details some of the pros and cons of a universal basic income and discusses how it contrasts with current forms of welfare policy such as income support and means-tested subsidies. Readers will learn how a universal basic income might help to combat the unemployment trap, showing for example, how a regular and guaranteed income could incentivize citizens to take more risks to find new work – without fear of losing welfare payments or having to reapply for them should their new employment not work out. Finland's basic income experiment (discussed in Chapter 4) is one example of a policy trial aimed at addressing their unemployment troubles. This text shows how a universal basic income might provide a stimulus to engage in remunerated work; replace means-tested subsidies, and remove disincentives to work. But the text shall also examine the downsides to a universal basic income, such as the potential difficulties in funding it; getting the public onside to support it, and how its implementation might impact on certain social groups. In Chapter 7 ('Against a universal basic income'), readers shall look at arguments which suggest that a universal basic income might exacerbate the sexual division of labour, having adverse effects on women in particular. The chapter will also examine how a universal basic income might lead to the tightening of border controls, leading to adverse effects for migrant workers. Readers shall also engage with a debate on whether or not a universal basic income can provide compensatory justice and re-shape lax welfare policies to ones which are more stringent. These discussions are laid out in Chapter 2 of this text, where a number of different theories and theorists are discussed, alongside some conventional philosophical debates around work, liberty and social justice (such as 'What is freedom?'). This chapter introduces how the idea of a universal basic income or citizen's income has emerged, examining some of the problems of a capitalist economic system, and showing how a universal basic income might be emancipatory and provide a redistributive safety net to all citizens of a given society. The chapter shall also lay out the general aims and objectives of the text on universal basic income and provides a breakdown and brief introduction of the forthcoming chapters in this book.

What is universal basic income?

What is a universal basic income? A universal basic income is a regular cash income paid to all on an individual basis, without means test or work requirement. The basic income is 'universal', because it is paid to all in a given community or society. Whether or not individuals are rich or poor, and regardless of whether or not they receive income from other sources, a universal basic income is paid to everyone by virtue of being a member or citizen of that community or society. It is for this reason that a universal basic income has also been referred to as a 'citizen's wage' or 'citizen's income' – 'an unconditional, automatic and non-withdrawable payment to each individual as a right of citizenship' (Torry, 2016). In various books and articles, a 'universal basic income' or 'basic income' has also been referred to as a 'existence income', 'universal dividend', 'universal grant', or 'guaranteed universal subsidy', as well as a range of similar terms in a variety of languages. Universal basic income may appear to be a far-flung idea, a utopian proposition, or ambitious set of policy ideas. In recent years, however, governments around the world have started putting this idea into practice.

Why is this topic so important? In recent years, the teaching of universal basic income in higher education is becoming more and more popular to an array of courses across the social sciences, including undergraduate degrees in social policy; sociology; education studies; economics; law; business; politics; social work and community studies. But students are not the only ones interested in understanding the debates about universal basic income. Human rights activists, community leaders, politicians, lawyers and business leaders also want to understand more about universal basic income. Universal basic income represents not simply a social policy or means of welfare, but a fundamental change in the way in which society is constructed and developed, so it draws upon the expertise and specialisms of scholars and practitioners from a vast range of subject areas and industries. Everybody, including those of you who are studying universal basic income for the first time, can contribute to this important debate.

Many see universal basic income as a policy which will radically change capitalist society as we know it. But universal basic income is not developed to dismantle capitalism. On the contrary, in most cases, the arguments put forward to implement a universal basic income are based on the idea that a basic income is needed in order to allow capitalist societies to survive and to work effectively. Capitalism, driven by neoliberal economics, is currently failing many in societies across the world. A universal basic income has the potential to rescue some of the shortcomings of neoliberal capitalist society, providing more security where very often there is none. But arguably, a universal basic income itself can be considered 'neoliberal', in the sense that it emphasizes individual choice and freedom, with only minimal interference from the state – though this is controversial.

So, what is the basic philosophy of a universal basic income? This question of course depends upon who is implementing a basic income and how it might be implemented and where. But current literature on universal basic income suggests that *there is* a basic philosophy – a nature, or set of basic ideas of what a universal basic income should be. First, a universal basic income is supported by those who believe that a fair and just society is possible – so it has a moral and ethical philosophy. Second, it has the potential to improve and replace current welfare provisions in many ways, such as *abolishing the stigma* associated with means-tested benefits, and solving the problems of the poverty and unemployment traps. Third, unlike the way in which many other welfare provisions are perceived, a universal basic income can be understood as an *investment in society*, rather than a cost. Take for example those who wish to change careers or start their own business. The risk involved in taking such bold decisions can arguably be minimized with the provision of a universal basic income. Another important aspect of a universal basic income is that it can enhance the mutual responsibility within a community or society because everyone is given the income by virtue of being a citizen. This in itself can support *social cohesion* and provide the basis of a strong community.

Providing a minimum income to every citizen can also provide *more freedom*. Recipients of a basic income are able to move more easily among paid work, education, caring and volunteering when there is a universal basic income. Rather than keeping people stuck in the jobs they may dislike, a universal basic income allows individuals to have *more autonomy* to choose the jobs they want, or move from one job to the next with less hassle and financial burden. Van Parijs and Vanderborght (2017: 26) argue that 'making an economy more productive (sensibly interpreted) in a sustainable fashion is not best served by obsessively activating people and locking them in jobs that they hate doing and from which they learn nothing'. But does a universal basic income assume the goodwill and good intentions of the individual recipient? Critics of a universal basic income suggest that a basic income will generate a culture of idleness, a reliance on the state, and a selfishness of individuals to squandering their money, for example, on alcohol and video entertainment. Many of these criticisms are banded about in public media, often without real substance or detailed evidence. But in *The Right to Exploit: Parasitivism, Scarcity, Basic Income*, author Gijs van Donselaar (2009) provides a more nuanced account of how the nature and value of freedom of choice can be understood. He argues that policies like a universal basic income can lead to exploitative relations. He shows how a universal basic income could license parasitic behaviour – bettering oneself by worsening another. And so, although the majority of real case studies and experiments of universal basic income discussed in this textbook show many positive outcomes, there are still many concerns of whether such a policy is morally right and whether it will work.

Experiments from various countries are still in the early stages, but research results show that recipients of genuine basic income pilots tend to invest in themselves, their families and the communities in which they live. Many examples show that money is not squandered, but used to improve important aspects of social life, including employment conditions, housing, education and healthcare (see Chapter 4 to read about the experiment in Madhya Pradesh, India, in which more than 6,000 people from twenty villages benefitted from a basic cash income). Some critics of a universal basic income often argue that it would disincentivize work – assuming that people on low incomes would not bother to work if receiving a 'comfortable' level of income. But rarely is the same said about the super-rich. After all, billionaires such as Bill Gates (Microsoft), Richard Branson (Virgin) and Mark Zuckerberg (Facebook) still work, though they do not need the income. A study of lottery winners (in 1999) found that most people continued to work (in one form or another) even after receiving large lottery payouts. Few were still in the same jobs they had before but most 'still worked' in some capacity (see Standing, 2017: 165). Paulsen's (2008) research found that when people were asked what they would do when winning the lottery, a clear majority said they would carry on working, though not necessarily in jobs they did before.

A universal basic income has the potential to radically reform welfare systems all over the world. Existing welfare systems often restricts what people can do and holds back their potential for developing themselves and their families in financial ways, and other ways too. A British woman (lone parent) in receipt of means-tested benefits (including tax credits) might hesitate to move in with (cohabitate) a partner (with earned income) because she would immediately lose her benefit income. An Indian woman living in a poor district of Uttar Pradesh must marry in order to pay for her children's school fees, if she wants a better life for her children, and whether or not she wants to marry. A universal basic income would arguably *free up* these constraints, and provide people with more autonomy over their own lives.

The emergence of a universal basic income

How has a universal basic income emerged? The idea of a universal basic income may have become more popular in recent years, but it is actually an old idea suggested at least two hundred years ago. In 1795, the English-born American activist Thomas Paine advocated a citizen's dividend to all US citizens as compensation for 'loss of his or her natural inheritance, by the introduction of the system of landed property' (Paine, 1795). More than 150 years later, Paine's sentiments were echoed by another revolutionary of his time. In 1967, during the Civil Rights Movement, Martin Luther King suggested that a guaranteed minimum income was the most simplest and effective way of abolishing poverty in the US, arguing for an end to social inequality and social justice for all. Less than ten years later, one US state created a policy which has resonance with the idea of a universal basic income, or citizen's income. In 1976, the state of Alaska created the Alaska Permanent Fund, a dividend paid to Alaska residents using oil revenues, one of Alaska's most abundant and rich resources. The fund may not exactly be what Thomas Paine or Martin Luther King had in mind, and has become a topic of discussion and scrutiny for Alaskan residents, but it has been, until recently, one model which has resonance with to the notion of a permanent and universal basic income.

Over the last twenty years however, the idea of a universal basic income has become increasingly popular, and more and more governments and NGOs (non-government organizations) all over the world have begun piloting and experimenting with the idea of a universal basic income (these pilots and experiments are discussed in Chapter 4 of this book). This popularity of universal basic income is not due to chance, but comes in response to a changing economic climate – one which has been based upon neoliberal economics, ideas and values. Current ideas about how economic and financial systems should work are rooted in a style of economics known as 'laissez-faire', or 'leave alone'. Free from the restrictions imposed on it by the state, the market can supposedly do as it pleases (see Friedman, 1962). Without state interference, the 'free market economy', as it is known, develop 'naturally' and freely, allowing capitalism to flourish and wealth to be created. Without the protections afforded to it by the state, however, these free markets have had dire consequences (or adverse side-effects) for societies (see Polanyi, 1944). Driven by neoliberal policies, these free market economies have been characterized by instability and adverse change. Rather than securing stable living conditions for families and individuals, a neoliberal economy creates uncertainty and fragility which can often lead to crisis. For example, in the pursuit of market efficiency, the labor markets of economies have become more and more deregulated. The removal of regulations or restrictions in industry has created an emerging culture of precarity in work and employment (Standing, 2015; McDonough, 2017). Precarious employment involves instability, lack of protection, insecurity and social or economic vulnerability (McDonough, 2017). One way this has happened has been the demise of traditional employment contracts (full-time and permanent) – replaced with short-term (often zero-hour) contracts. Known as the 'Burger King contract' (named after the multinational chain Burger King, infamous for employing to low skill and low paid jobs) employers are increasingly using precarious contracts of employment often without a guaranteed set number of hours each week – 'resulting in the pure casualization of labour' (McDonough, 2017: 99). This kind of contract has been implemented in all sectors of work, including universities, hospitals, schools and a plethora of private companies and multinational organizations. In this textbook, we outline the notion of precariousness (see Chapter 3), examining how a universal basic income intends to resolve the problems caused by this uncertainty – such as providing a steady resource which counterbalances the unsteadiness of precarity and the gig economy.

Contemporary capitalist societies are driven by neoliberal imperatives which, by their very nature, create a number of adverse side-effects, including: uncertainty; insecurity; poverty, and social inequalities. A universal basic income has emerged as a response to these side effects. It can reduce uncertainty because it is a regular and therefore constant resource available for use. It can also provide a basic security, because it is a sustained income which takes families above the poverty line and is provided continuously. Having a stable and certain income provides a stability and assurance which allows individuals and families the time and resources to plan their future, giving them the means with which to provide self-improvement, escaping poverty and acquiring a better quality of life.

Universal basic income: a progressive social policy?

A universal basic income is seen as a progressive policy in several ways. First, it provides a secure financial foundation on which all members of society would be free to build upon. It would help to reduce or eliminate poverty by providing every citizen with an income regardless of capital they possess (property, for example) or income they receive from family (parental income or inheritance, for example). It can improve living standards in relation to wide range of factors including health and nutrition, housing, schooling and education. Second, a universal basic income is a policy which goes beyond welfare in the sense that it can also contribute to growth, by raising productivity, creating a more sustainable platform for work and the development of income. Third, a universal basic income is *emancipatory* (if implemented correctly). It is a means of enhancing, or in some cases reclaiming, personal freedom or basic rights. A universal basic income has the potential to be particularly emancipatory for women (see Chapter 5), and those who normally receive lower priority in social policymaking, including those with disabilities or the elderly (Devala et al., 2015). However, some critics believe that people will squander their money on bad habits, or what Standing (2017: 79) calls 'private bads'. There is an underlying discourse which depicts poorer people in society as untrustworthy and irresponsible. Giving people an unconditional income could result in money being wasted on alcohol, drugs and other 'private bads'. Standing (2017) argues however, that the evidence from current basic income pilots points in the opposite direction – for the most part, recipients of basic income or cash transfer programmes spend their money on 'private goods'. Standing (2017) argues that contrary to popular prejudice, studies show that basic income is more likely to be spent on food for children, family healthcare, and education. Standing (2017) further expands this argument by saying that receipt of a universal basic income can actually *reduce* spending on drugs, alcohol and tobacco. Because a universal basic income can reduce poverty and radically alter a hopeless situation, it can also change the mind-set of families and entire communities. A shift in the way in which people understand their situation can reduce the need to alleviate a difficult and hopeless situation by turning to alcohol and drug misuse.

The idea of a universal basic income is very controversial. First, why should a basic income get paid (to everyone) universally? If a basic income aims to eradicate poverty then why not target the poorest in society? One reason is that benefits targeted at the poor often require those eligible to take steps which they may fail to take, whether out of 'ignorance, shyness, or shame'(Van Parijs and Vanderborght, 2017: 17). With a means-tested scheme there are considerably more human and administrative costs than with a universal basic income. Furthermore, the means-test itself is problematic. Decisions to include or exclude can 'leave a lot of room for arbitrariness and clientelism' (Van Parijs and Vanderborght, 2017: 18). Unlike other welfare schemes, there is no stigma attached to receiving a basic income when it is the right of *every* citizen. But it is not only the dignity of people which is afforded by a universal basic income. Such a scheme would also enhance the effectiveness of poverty alleviation. By avoiding complication and stigmatization, a universal basic income can 'achieve a high rate of take-up at a low information cost' (Van Parijs and Vanderborght, 2017: 18). There are other reasons why a universal basic income might be better than welfare policies targeted at the poor. In a neoliberal economy where work is often characterized by insecurity and precariousness (McDonough, 2017), a universal basic income not only frees people from a lack of money, but also provides more flexibility for individuals to take on work they require. As Van Parijs and Vanderborght argue:

> if they are unsure about how much they will earn when they start working, about whether they will be able to cope, or about how quickly they might lose the work and then have to face more or less complex administrative procedures in order to reestablish their entitlement to benefits, the idea of giving up means-tested transfers holds less appeal.
>
> *(Van Parijs and Vanderborght, 2017: 17–18)*

Under present welfare arrangements, in many countries, it can take several weeks of form-filling and administrative work to sign up someone to the correct benefits based upon their specific circumstances. The prospect of signing-off and losing benefits is a disincentive to work. By contrast, with a universal basic income, people can take on jobs with less fear.

One of the most significant differences a universal basic income makes is the avoidance of the 'poverty trap' or 'unemployment trap'. This problem often occurs with current benefit systems, whereby an increase in someone's income through employment is offset by a consequent loss of state benefits, and set of costs involved in employment activity (travel or nanny costs, for instance). Torry (2016) for example, cites the example of a British carpenter who has been promoted to the position of foreman – and then wished he had not been. His wages had risen, but the effects of additional Income Tax and National Insurance Contributions, and the loss of Family Income Supplement (as the means-tested benefit was then called) resulted in the man being no better off. Linked to this problem, is the scale of government deductions from additional earnings of those who receive welfare benefits and are also active in the labour market (whether it is part-time or full-time work). Torry (2016) describes this situation in the UK:

> In the UK, a family receiving Housing Benefit, Council Tax Support, Working Tax Credits, and with the main breadwinner earning enough to be paying Income Tax and National Insurance Contributions, can find that each extra £1 that they earn will benefit the family's net income by just 4p. This is because Income Tax and National Insurance Contributions will be deducted from each additional £1 earned, and the additional earnings will cause means-tested benefits (in this case, Working Tax Credits, Child Tax Credits, Housing Benefit, and Council Tax Support) to be reduced.
>
> *(Torry, 2016: 62)*

The taxes in Britain all contribute to the infrastructure of British society: a free national healthcare service, free education, the police, the judiciary, and transport systems. All of these are essential to British society and its economy. But when the wealthiest in Britain pay to the government 47p of every extra £1 that they earn, compared with 96p for every extra £1 earned by the lowest earners, there is something amiss with the system (Torry, 2016).

In stark contrast to current welfare provisions, a universal basic income is not withdrawn or reduced when individuals find work because it is applicable to all, regardless of income. Rather than making the often daunting leap straight from means-tested welfare benefits into work, recipients of a universal basic income will have nothing to fear, for the basic income is continuous and obligation free. Current welfare systems in developed nations usually require countless hours filling out forms with personal information and involve continuously collecting data to support evidence that recipients are 'honest' in their claims. Aside from the high costs to implement this, are the costs involved in investigating those who have tried to dupe the system by making false claims for welfare. Governments often outsource work to private companies to carry out the administrative functions of the welfare system. In the UK for example, companies such as Serca, Capita (a leading outsourcing business for professional services), G4S (a leading supplier of security solutions and other services), Pertemps and Seetec are paid millions of pound in order to enforce welfare regimes in Britain. The implementation of a universal basic income might eliminate the need for corporate outsourcing which drains the welfare budget and diverts the money which should be helping all members of society. However, the administration for a universal basic income could be outsourced too, depending on how it is implemented.

Can a universal basic income benefit women? When governments slash spending on welfare provision it is always women who lose out most. In Britain, for example, more than 70% of tax credits and more than 90% of child benefits go to women. Reductions to welfare spend can have dire consequences for women in particular, which can exacerbate gender inequalities, and often make women more reliant on men within the family. In contrast to means-tested welfare provisions, supporters of a universal basic income argue that it can provide 'liberty' (Torry, 2016) or 'freedom' (Devala et al., 2015), particularly for women, because it provides more autonomy over life choices. For example, women are able to choose the kinds of employment patterns which suit their needs, allowing the flexibility to take up short-term or part-time work, without the additional income affecting the amount of welfare benefits they receive – a drawback with means-tested benefits. In Britain, like other countries around the globe, having children can put a great deal of strain on families, with some women feeling that having a baby is a burden. A working woman who has children must sacrifice her income to raise her child. A universal basic income will of course not match the paid income from paid work, but it can compensate those who wish to drop employment, for the important 'work' of raising children. This of course is more beneficial to women (and arguably to society more broadly), who are still more likely than men to have child caring responsibilities. However, it is easy to see why some feminists may be sceptical of a universal basic income – it is only good for women if we assume that more women will be the ones at home looking after the children and taking care of domestic responsibilities. Policies that seemingly support women can at the same time reinforce the caring roles of women and exacerbate the sexual division of labour (as discussed later in Chapters 5 and 7).

One of the biggest problems with the current means-tested benefits in developed nations is the way in which it is perceived by the public. People often oppose the idea of 'hand-outs' from the state, or the use of taxes to be given to those who seem too lazy or idle to work. A universal basic income, however, is paid to everyone, so there is no envy or strong opposition to those who receive it, when it is a provision for all. A good example of this is the National Health Service (hereafter, the NHS) in Britain. Because it is free at the point of use for all in the UK, it has very strong public support across the political spectrum. A survey of 1,111 people carried out in 2017 by the Institute for Policy Research at the University of Bath found that 49% of British people aged 18 to 75 years old generally supported the introduction of a universal basic income. However, support for the scheme dropped to 30% when people were asked to consider universal basic income funding through increased taxation. Luke Martinelli (2017) argues that the data show 'surprising levels of support for basic income in the UK – although this falls when asked to consider UBI's fiscal implications'. The research also found that those leaning politically to the left were more likely to support the scheme than those who lean towards the right, with 63% of Labour Party-leaning adults supporting the principle of universal basic income, compared with 40% of those who are Conservative Party-leaning.

Motivating people to work has for a long time been a matter of simultaneously incentivizing and threatening. This contradictory approach simply does not work. The problems with the welfare state were best illustrated in British movie director Ken Loach's film *I, Daniel Blake* (2017), in which a 59-year-old joiner called Daniel Blake is depicted as a victim of the British system of work and welfare, in which he is sent from 'pillar to post' in order to make ends meet when he loses his long-term job. Having suffered a heart attack, Blake is instructed by doctors to rest. But because he is able to walk 50 metres and able to raise either arm to his top shirt pocket, the welfare state considers him 'fit for work' and send him on a number of CV writing workshops and classes in order to find work. The film depicts the British welfare regime as a cruel system that stigmatizes unemployment and vilifies people for not having a job. Blake eventually dies. And so, a universal basic income is not just a policy aimed at alleviating poverty but can also be seen as a progressive policy for overcoming the necessity to means-test, degrade and devalue citizens who are unemployed.

Social inequalities and universal basic income

Equality is one of the key reasons for implementing a universal basic income. But what is 'equality'? In most discussions on universal basic income, equality refers to the rights or equal opportunities to live in a society which is fair and just in a myriad of ways. Equality refers to having equal rights politically, economically and socially. Under a capitalist system however, many aspects of equality are hindered by capitalist values – arguably dictated by the rich and powerful. For example, in Tony Atkinson's (2015) *Inequality: What Can Be Done?*, the author examines how the wealthy disproportionately influence public policy and influence governments to implement policies that protect wealth of the ruling elite. Take for example tax avoidance by multi-national corporations, such as the internet giant Google and the coffee chain Starbucks, who have entered markets of countries all around the world but managed to avoid paying tax in so many of them. Unlike many ordinary citizens whose tax is deducted automatically from their wages, large corporations can negotiate the tax they pay, or invest in teams of accountants to lawfully avoid paying out any tax altogether. Many multinationals have 'parent' or 'sister' companies which can offload expenses, or use loop holes to move money around in a way which permits them to operate without the need to pay tax in a given location. Many of these parent companies are registered in offshore tax havens, such as the Isle of Man (off the coast of England), or parts of the Caribbean. The avoidance of tax by the rich and powerful is just one example of inequality in capitalist society. Advocating for a basic income, Atkinson (2015) argues that government interventions are required to provide better equality across society, by ensuring that there is a fairer distribution of wealth for example.

The issue of equality is taken up by social researchers Wilkinson and Pickett, in their key text *The Spirit Level: Why Equality is Better for Everyone*. Wilkinson and Pickett (2011) argue that a plethora of social issues, from life expectancy, to poor housing and healthcare, to obesity, illiteracy and violence are not affected by how wealthy a society is, but how equal it is. Drawing on years of empirical research from data on countries around the world, Wilkinson and Pickett (2011) found that societies with a bigger gap between the richest and poorest are some of the worst for social problems and social issues which affect everyone (the rich and the poor). Using a variety of sociological measures, the authors found that countries with a smaller gap between the wealthiest and poorest in society tended to be 'happier', 'healthier', with a better standing of living for all. Countries with the largest gaps between the rich and poor (such as Britain and the US) tended to suffer from chronic social problems. There is also concern that precarious work is accelerated by an increasing gap between the richest and poorest in society (Standing, 2015). Wilkinson and Pickett (2011) show that this is no coincidence, but that there is a direct link between wealth distribution and the health, lifestyle conditions and wellbeing of communities living within that country.

More recently, in 2019, Wilkinson and Pickett published *The Inner Level: How More Equal Societies Reduce Stress, Restore Sanity and Improve Everyone's Well-being*. In this key text, Wilkinson and Pickett (2019) show how inequality affects individuals, and that material inequalities have powerful effects on the ways in which individuals feel, think and behave. One of the important perceptions they challenge is the idea that people are naturally driven by competition and self-interest. Societies with more equality, sharing and reciprocity are more likely to provide a healthier, less stressful and more positive environment and wellbeing for the individuals who live there. Overall, Wilkinson and Pickett (2011, 2019) find that countries with bigger income differences between rich and poor, tend to suffer from lower life expectancy; higher rates of homicide and suicide; worse physical and mental health conditions; worse problems with drug dealing and drug abuse; poorer literacy among the young, and higher rates of crime with more people incarcerated. These arguments are useful for understanding the benefits of a universal basic income, which could be used as a way of tackling some of the problems brought about by wealth inequalities in societies around the world.

Summary

Across the globe, universal basic income is gaining momentum as a philosophy and social policy, which can bring about positive social change and social equality. But universal basic income is not some ad hoc idea without sound and robust foundations. On the contrary, a universal basic income rests upon a number of philosophical foundations and underlying theories. These foundations are laid out in Chapter 2 of this text, examining the underpinning theories and philosophical positions of universal basic income, and analysing how these ideas might support and provide a fairer society. Among other perspectives, the chapter draws on John Rawls's (1971) *A Theory of Justice* and Van Parijs's (1997) *Real Freedom for All: What (if anything) Can Justify Capitalism?* to understand notions of equality, social justice and freedom and examine how these ideas might support a universal basic income. The chapter also draws upon Marxist theory through commentary on the work of Gorz (1999) to show the systematic problems of capitalist society and how different approaches have given rise to the idea of a universal basic income.

In the third chapter, this textbook addresses precarious work and the social inequalities it creates. Against the backdrop of Guy Standing's (2015, 2017) works and other contemporary perspectives that lay foundations for a universal income, this chapter examines how a basic income can address the precarious nature of work and the social inequalities and insecurities this creates. By drawing upon several examples from different sectors of workers who might benefit from a universal basic income, this chapter also describes the inequalities experienced by those who suffer from the economic effects of neoliberalism – precarious workers who are subject to insecure, unprotected and poorly paid working conditions. It maps out how a universal basic income can remedy some of the problems of precarious and insecure forms of employment and livelihood.

Chapter 4 examines several examples and experiments of universal basic income. It includes the case of Finland, one of the first countries in Europe to launch a universal basic income pilot, in which, over a two-year period, 2,000 unemployed citizens between the ages of 25 and 58 received 560 euros a month. The chapter also looks at the case of Alaska, an oil rich state of the USA, in which a Permanent Fund Dividend (PFD) is paid to Alaska residents living within the state – a minimum salary distributed to every citizen, regardless of age, employment, or social standing. Another example of basic income this chapter examines is an 'experiment' based in Madhya Pradesh, India, in which more than six thousand people from twenty villages benefitted from a basic cash income. The chapter also examines other historical and contemporary experiments examples from around the world. Using real examples, and contrasting how a universal basic income might work in different kinds of nations, this chapter looks at the varied effects a basic income has on the poor and wealthy; unemployed and working; young and old and those who are privileged and under-privileged.

In Chapter 5, universal basic income is examined in relation to the work, roles and status of women. With an emphasis on laying out a feminist economics perspective to raise the issue of a universal basic income, the chapter explores several examples and test-cases in which basic income has been implemented and changed the economic and social experiences of women in various social contexts. In some of these cases discussed, the chapter explores how a basic income can provide women with financial dependence, allowing them a new means of 'freedom'. But the implementation of a universal basic income can have varying effects on women from diverse social class and ethnic backgrounds. This chapter will discuss the potential a universal basic income has in promoting equal rights for men and women and how this would challenge the institutionalized and disadvantaged relationship between work and welfare as experienced by women of different ethnicities and social class positions.

Chapter 6 examines how universal basic income might help the environment by helping to reduce the 'carbon footprint'. In this chapter, the notion of sustainable consumption is presented as an alternative to counteract the consumer attitudes and choices which give rise to patterns of consumption adversely affecting the natural environment. This chapter shows how a universal basic income can change consumerist mind-sets and behaviour, as well as changing our perceptions towards work. Mapping out the new green agenda in politics and wider society, we show how universal basic income has been advocated by green parties across Europe and the rest of the world, explaining how green politicians think a basic income policy would help rescue the environment. The chapter also looks at the implications of eco-taxes and how this could help fund a universal basic income.

A universal basic income is approached from a very different perspective in Chapter 7. Examining some of the key problems with a universal basic income, this chapter focusses on arguments against a universal basic income, explaining difficulties which might arise from its implementation. This chapter will explore the financial costs associated with a universal basic income provision; the incentive or disincentives to work; the notion of parasitism – living at another person's expense; the expansion of the nanny-state and the attack against freedom, and the alternatives to a universal basic income which could arguably provide more freedom. Drawing on several different economic and political perspectives, this chapter examines the pitfalls of a universal basic income and shows how a universal basic income can be problematic and may disadvantage certain social groups, such as 'non-citizens' or migrant workers.

The final chapter reflects upon a universal basic income, evaluating arguments for and against a universal basic income by revisiting some of the key examples discussed in previous chapters. Drawing on real examples of welfare implementation, the chapter highlights some of the fundamental advantages and difficulties, of putting a universal basic income into practice. For those readers who are studying basic income for the first time, the concluding chapter offers an avenue to reflect on your own learning, and revise the overall debates which have been presented throughout the entire textbook.

References

Atkinson, A. B. (2015) *Inequality: What Can Be Done?* Cambridge, MA: Harvard University Press.

Devala, S., Jhabvala, R., Mehta, S. K. and Standing, G. (2015) *Basic Income: A Transformative Policy for India*. London: Bloomsbury. Friedman, M. (1962) *Capitalism and Freedom*. Chicago, IL: University of Chicago Press.

Gorz, A. (1999) *Reclaiming Work: Beyond a Wage Based Society*. Cambridge: Cambridge Policy Press.

King, M. L. (1967) *Where Do We Go from Here: Chaos or Community?* Boston, MA: Beacon Press.

Martinelli, L. (2017) *The Fiscal and Distributional Implications of Alternative Universal Basic Income Schemes in the UK*. Bath: Institute for Policy Research, University of Bath.

McDonough, B. (2017) 'Precarious work and unemployment in Europe'. In: S. Isaacs, ed. *European Social Problems*. London: Routledge.

Paine, T. (1795) 'Agrarian justice'. In: T. Paine, *Common Sense with Agrarian Justice*. London: Penguin.

Paulsen, R. (2008) 'Economically forced to work: A critical reconsideration of the lottery question'. *Basic Income Studies*, 3(2), pp. 1–20.

Polanyi, K. (1944) *The Great Transformation: The Political and Economic Origins of our Time*. Boston, MA: Beacon Press.

Rawls, J. (1971) *A Theory of Justice*. Cambridge, MA: Harvard University Press.

Standing, G. (2015) *The Precariat: A New Dangerous Class*. London: Penguin.

Standing, G. (2017) *Basic Income: And How We Can Make It Happen*. London: Penguin.

Torry, M. (2016) *Citizen's Basic Income: A Christian Social Policy*. London: Darton, Longman and Todd.

Van Donselaar, G. (2009) *The Right to Exploit: Parasitism, Scarcity, Basic Income*. Oxford: Oxford University Press.

Van Parijs, P. (1997) *Real Freedom for All: What (if anything) Can Justify Capitalism?* Oxford: Clarendon Press.

Van Parijs, P. and Vanderborght, Y. (2017) *Basic Income: A Radical Proposal for a free Society and a Sane Economy*: Cambridge, MA: Harvard University Press.

Wilkinson, R. and Pickett, K. (2011) *The Spirit Level: Why Equality is Better for Everyone*. London: Bloomsbury.

Wilkinson, R. and Pickett, K. (2019) *The Inner Level: How More Equal Societies Reduce Stress, Restore Sanity and Improve Everyone's Well-being*. London: Penguin.

2

UNDERPINNING THEORIES AND PHILOSOPHICAL POSITIONS OF UNIVERSAL BASIC INCOME

Introduction

We can better understand universal basic income if we examine the theories and philosophical positions that underpin it. Drawing on debates around inequality, freedom and social justice, this chapter explores a range of theories, theoretical concepts and philosophical approaches to universal basic income. Among other theories and approaches connected to *social inequality* this chapter draws on Marxist perspectives to map out the influence they have on understanding the problems of social inequalities in a capitalist society and the potential a universal basic income has of tackling them. This is followed by a discussion about *freedom*, drawing on Philippe Van Parijs's ideas about freedom and liberty from his book *Real Freedom for All: What (if anything) Can Justify Capitalism?* (Van Parijs, 1997). Van Parijs's is used to ground an understanding of freedom in a society that is naturally coercive and how a universal basic income can promote a greater sense of liberty. Later, this chapter examines the notion of *social justice*, by discussing John Rawls's *A Theory of Justice* (Rawls, 1999), addressing how social justice and a universal basic income can be compatible. Finally, there is a critical commentary reflecting on the importance of analysing a universal basic income through theories and approaches around equality, freedom and social justice. In all, this chapter aims to provide readers with a grasp of the key ideas that revolve around a number of contentious issues debated within and integral to, some *key principles* of universal basic income: importance of equality in a capitalist society; notion of freedom for all, and the idea of social justice.

Social inequality and universal basic income

One underlying principle of a universal basic income revolves around the idea of social equality. Across Europe and many parts of the globe, social equality 'underpins public policy and is recognition of the fundamental rights of all citizens' (Clark, 2002: 18). But 'equality' and 'inequality' can mean 'different things to different people' (Atkinson, 2015: 2). For example, we can examine inequality of opportunity or inequality of outcome; inequality of political power, or economic inequality. All of these forms of inequality matter though we sometimes put more emphasis on some more than others. In many debates on universal basic income, equality refers to the rights or equal opportunities to live in a society which is fair and just, having equal rights politically, economically and socially. Social inequality occurs when resources are unevenly distributed, when rights are violated and when opportunities are not equally accessible to all. One of the most important ways in which governments decide how equality is distributed is through people's engagement in work. Think about how we are encouraged and trained from schooling to take up jobs, how taxes are collected from our salary to pay for services, how employed citizens are regarded as enjoying the better benefits a society can offer, and also how those not employed are regarded to be excluded or at risk of exclusion. Thus, within our system there is a direct link between work and pay; the idea behind a universal basic income would be to break this link and reclaim the notion of work. Following Marxist perspectives, this section examines the potential of basic income to redefine the notion of work and to bring about more equality in society.

Debates around a universal basic income call into question taken-for-granted notions that make up everyday life, such as work. The idea of a universal basic income has provoked considerable interest due to how it could help respond to traditionalistic political and economic regimes based on capitalist relations and the problems with ideas around work. Marxism provides a useful critique of 'work' in capitalist society, by illuminating how it seemingly offers rewards to those who 'work hard' and punishes those who do not, or who are not owners of capital. Interestingly, those who do own substantial capital, the wealthy, need not work at all. There is no pressure on them to 'get out of bed' and to go into work. Marx himself outlined a contradiction between the lives of the ruling class, the bourgeoisie, and the working class masses whose labour is exploited for profit. To better understand the exploitative relations between the ruling elite and the working classes, Marx outlined the mode of production, in which productive forces (human labour power) and the means of production (machinery; tools; infrastructure, technical knowledge) combined to enable the production of goods and use of services. Importantly, Marx also highlighted the relations of production (property, power and control) which marked the ways in which the ruling elite maintained ways of exploiting the working classes for their labour. In the *Economic and Philosophic Manuscripts of 1844*, Marx used the term 'alienation' to describe the estranged feeling workers had from the products of their labour, as well as their own creativity (Marx, 2007). In Marx's view, people were alienated from their full human potential. It is this Marxist idea in particular, which makes universal basic income so appealing. By providing a standard cash sum, no strings attached, people will be more empowered to choose jobs which they feel fit with their human potential, rather than being forced into work where they will encounter alienation.

Capitalism is a system developed to produce profit, not to benefit the mass members of society. For this reason, Marxist philosophers and economists such as Andre Gorz (1923–2007) argue that we must have a system which goes beyond a wage based society. Within a capitalist system, work is seen as paid employment, and not the 'real work' people do in everyday life, even when they're not formally employed: caring and cleaning for others; raising the next generation; voluntary, community and other non-paid work. In his book *Reclaiming Work: Beyond a Wage-Based Society*, Gorz (1999: 2) argues for an end to work which is peculiar to capitalist society. When we say to a certain woman that 'she doesn't work' when she is raising her children, but 'she does work' if that same woman is a paid nanny or nursery school worker we are strengthening the divisions around work in our society. Gorz's (1999) critique of work is also founded on how Marx viewed the mode of production of societies influencing social meanings in all aspects of society, from culture and education, to the world of work everything is designed to serve the purposes of the particular mode of production. In the case of capitalism, work is reduced to the exchange of labour for a wage, workers are reduced to wage earners, and work can only be supplied to the economic institutions which have gained recognition in capitalism. Consequently, any situation which does not resemble these structures cannot possibly be viewed as real work.

Yet, this interpretation of real work must incorporate the wide scope of human activity, rather than being limited to those things we do during paid employment. Gorz (1999) argues that we should try to produce a system which provides a decent livelihood for all, a system of basic income. Gorz is not interested in a minimum income, which provides merely subsistence, or participation income, which requires some condition of a person participating in care work (or other activity). Gorz (1999) wants an unconditional and universal basic income which is adequate enough for a decent level of subsistence. Only a basic income can recompense the voluntary, community, caring and non-market activities of which society depends. Furthermore, a basic income would make real the notion of 'inclusion' by bringing together members of society and providing greater equality. Gorz (1999: 54) asks us to recognize that 'neither the right to an income, nor full citizenship, nor everyone's sense of identity and self-fulfilment can any longer be centred on and depend on occupying a job'. Therefore, the introduction of a universal basic income could widen the interpretations around work that we currently hold as a society. Universal basic income could contribute to the creation of more comprehensive and egalitarian social arrangements where work is not solely validated when a person is working for a wage, but instead recognizing that the majority of people in society do important work that sustains the way we live.

Capitalist social and economic relations enable a certain level of conditions which underpin the wellbeing and the freedoms individuals in society can enjoy. In society, we normally regard an individual as being able to engage fully if they have a place within the means of production of a society. For the vast majority of us, our place in the mode of production of capitalism means we are employees, individuals who sell our labour. Millions of people go to work every day not just because they want to, or because they might draw satisfaction from what they do, but rather because they need to. From a Marxist perspective these values exist within a capitalist mode of production and are always shaped by class conflict. An introduction to universal basic income would be incomplete without incorporating some reflections on how the introduction of an unconditional, regular payment to individuals might affect the relations of power and class struggles between workers and employers in capitalist economies.

Within Marxist thought the logic of capitalism is critiqued through the intellectual tool of class analysis, in other words capitalism thrives on class conflict (Dahms, 2015). The worker without work and without a wage is a dispossessed individual in society; the worker needs to sell his/her labour if he/she is to buy the sustenance necessary to live in society. Yet, the very sustenance bought by workers is the preservation and maintenance of capitalist systems which exist in unequal social relations. The worker only has his/her labour to sell, and very often that labour is sold under prevailing economic systems based on exploitation and insecurity. This is exacerbated in an employment market where employers' rights are being eroded constantly, with the disempowering of trade unions, the rise of insecure work due to technological advancements, zero hour contracts and the widening gap between the rich and the poor (Standing, 2015; Pitts et al., 2017). The rise of job insecurity has been disguised by a significant rise in self-employment which in most cases precludes basic employment rights, such as the right to a minimum wage, sick pay, pension contributions, and parental leave, 'self-employment grew by 47% between 2000 and 2017 … This rise has mainly been among lower skilled workers, with average self-employed earnings now 20 per cent lower today than ten years ago' (Harrop and Tait, 2017: 9). Such factors compose the class conflict of our current societies. Capitalist social relations ensure that the worker is enslaved to his/her wage, while pay stagnates and profit rises, capitalism is allowed to fulfil its primary purpose, the production of money, of ever-accumulating profit, 'its aim is abstract wealth as such: capitalism is production for production's sake' (Bellofiore, 2009: 282). Thus, it is important to ask how in this historical period of rapidly accumulating profit, how an economic measure such as universal basic income can help change the dynamics of class conflict between workers and employers?

Arguably, universal basic income can help disrupt unequal labour power relations and increase the bargaining power of workers. This becomes more important in current societies where the rise of insecurity and uncertainty has grown proportionally with the rise of unequal accumulations of wealth globally (Piketty, 2014). The position of workers is becoming more precarious across different countries and different types of industry (Standing, 2015; McDonough, 2017). It is becoming increasingly more difficult to secure forms of employment that guarantee basic rights and benefits for workers and a salary with which an individual can have access to decent housing, services, leisure, health and other activities. Governments globally responded to these inequalities with a blind faith in the project of the 'knowledge economy' very broadly defined as 'an economy that is directly based on the production, distribution, and use of knowledge and information' (OECD, 1996). In order to secure these new types of employment which valued creativity and innovations in industry workers needed to have higher levels of education and a more entrepreneurial attitude at work. The knowledge economy as a project has proven as susceptible to economic chaos as any other economic project; this is evident in the rises in job insecurity and unemployment left by the economic crisis that hit the world in 2008 and which has left enduring patterns of inequality ever since (Švarc and Dabić, 2017).

While governments remain committed to the project of the knowledge economy by trying to triangulate knowledge, learning and business for economic growth and the creation of innovative and commercially viable services, there is still a continuing rise of uncertainty and insecurity in the very jobs offered by the knowledge economy (Wilczyńska et al., 2018). This is partly because the emergence of the knowledge economy took shape in political times which were pushing deregulation and the opening up of labour markets to allow for neoliberal projects of government to thrive. This 'has eased the lowering of wages' and increased competition for jobs in a labour market which was already affected by economic crises (Manjarin and Szlinder, 2016: 55).

The introduction of a universal basic income could increase the bargaining power of workers and offer a healthier solution to the unemployment experienced by people in society (Standing, 2017), offering insecure jobs to the unemployed is a common occurrence with people working on zero-hour contracts which threaten employment rights. Firstly, universal basic income could improve the current fears that workers feel about losing their jobs, or having to go into less stable jobs (Harrop and Tait, 2017). Unemployment in society helps drive down wages and working conditions; the awareness in people's minds that there is a substantial group of unemployed people in society subjugates workers into accepting less paid jobs or demand better working conditions (Manjarin and Szlinder, 2016). With the security of a universal basic income workers would be more willing to struggle for employment rights and better pay, as well as being able to study the market to secure better job opportunities, without the fear of losing the economic sustenance they need for themselves, or for their families. Secondly, the guarantee of a universal basic income could also create more 'collective bargaining power' (Manjarin and Szlinder, 2016: 54), whereby workers could be more encouraged to exercise their right to strike and support trade unions or workers' rights cooperatives.

The basic security offered by a universal basic income strengthens workers' position in front of the apparatus of capitalism at both an individual level and at a collective level. The conditions for these benefits to materialize also need to involve a political climate in which the basic rights of citizens do not become attacked on other fronts. For example, the amount paid as universal basic income should compensate individuals at a level where the expected minimum cost of living is met; if this payment is inadequate then the benefits to individuals or collective powers of workers would not occur as described. Equally, government policies which propose the retreat of state involvement in favour of the privatization of services and the reduction of the social wage or welfare state could also threaten the positive effects a universal basic income could have on workers. The social wage is the amount of government expenditure which is spent per person on public services, such as, social housing, healthcare and education. Imagine for a moment that you are in receipt of universal basic income but some of the services that were free before, such as seeing a doctor when feeling unwell, now become paid for by the individual. If basic services which did not incur any charge for individuals in society, such as sending your children to school, or accessing private and expensive health services – paid for by families and individuals, the introduction of a universal basic income would fail. Therefore, a certain level of commitment by governments to maintain a fair social wage to fund free services available to all citizens and which are not means-tested across health, education and welfare would be necessary for a universal basic income to remain positively impactful on workers' lives.

The notion of freedom and universal basic income

The notion of freedom is integral to discussions about a universal basic income. Many of those advocating for a universal basic income see it as a means for people to *attain freedom*. This might involve becoming free from poverty; freedom from exploitative employers; freedom to choose a suitable job, and/or the freedom to care for children or the very old or disabled without living below the poverty line. Universal basic income has the potential to unleash freedom from this perspective. On the other hand, critics of a universal basic income see it as an *infringement of our freedom* (or liberty), since we as tax payers are usually forced to pay into a large pot used to resource the basic income. From this perspective, a universal basic income can also limit our choices; encourage us not to work; enslave us to a nanny state system and discourage us from pursuing higher wages or becoming entrepreneurial. To understand the complexity of these arguments we need to better make sense of the notion of freedom.

A very influential perspective on freedom and important proposal around universal basic income is the one put forward by Philippe Van Parijs in his book *Real Freedom for All: What (if anything) Can Justify Capitalism?* Van Parijs presents a case for what he calls 'real libertarianism' (Van Parijs, 1997: 5), through his analysis of the abundant inequalities that can be found in capitalist societies and the constraining idea that we must always choose from pure capitalism or pure socialism. As we shall see in this section, Van Parijs discusses how libertarians have created a concept of the state based on the creation of rights and a system that can protect and reinforce these rights in society, in contrast

Van Parijs calls himself a 'real libertarian' (Van Parijs, 1997: 6), by not just upholding the importance of rights, but also very importantly, the involvement and engagement in these rights, as we will explain later in this section. Van Parijs (1997: 5) also proposes to 'distinguish capitalism from socialism in terms of whether the bulk of a society's means of production is privately or publicly owned'. Freedom is made compatible with equality in Van Parijs's analysis by pursuing a conceptualization of real-freedom-for-all which he debates is possible if the notion of a free society is not so closely tied to what society decides to be 'good' for citizens, but also how citizens can have access and experience these 'good' things society has to offer.

Van Parijs begins his analysis of libertarianism by suggesting that a free society, which can be understood as a society where its citizens enjoy the greatest extent of freedom, should not only base its ideal of freedom on '*formal freedom*' but on '*real-freedom-for-all*':

> Libertarians persuasively argue that no consistent formulation of the ideal of a free society can help giving a crucial role to a consistent system of private property rights. But by no means does it follow that only capitalism, let alone only pure capitalism, can be just. For there are many ways in which such a system of rights can be generated apart from the 'purely historical' one which libertarians favour. Put differently, libertarians rightly stress the importance of formal freedom, but formal freedom does not exhaust the real freedom that must feature in any defensible ideal of a free society ... 'real-freedom-for-all' is what really matters.
>
> *(Van Parijs, 1997: 5)*

Van Parijs's egalitarian ideal is trying to bring closer ideas around freedom as formally defined by the state and its institutions and the idea of freedom as the individual freedoms that a person might choose to enact. Think about how in society you might have rights which give you a determined scope of action to participate in society, however, through a lack of means you struggle to participate in the exercise of that right, this is still a curtail to your freedom. One good example which tends to gain some attention in the media is that of our right to own property, citizens can all own property, yet, many financial, social and historical inequalities prevent people from doing so. For Van Parijs, real freedom goes beyond formal freedom in that it allows individuals to do what they want to do, and not just what the moral duties or the preferred duties of a society dictates:

> Formal freedom can only be restricted by coercion, broadly understood as the (threat of a) violation of a person's rights, her ownership of herself included. But real freedom can be further restricted by any limit to what a person is permitted or enabled to do. Both a person's purchasing power and a person's genetic set-up, for example, are directly relevant to a person's real freedom. Unlike formal freedom, in other words, real freedom is not only a matter of having the right to do what one might want to do, but also a matter of having the means for doing it.
>
> *(Van Parijs, 1997: 5)*

Here, Van Parijs argues that real freedom accounts for *the means* of doing things in society which formal freedom cannot guarantee. The ways in which Van Parijs describes a free society also relate to ideas of justice. First, a free and just society must have a well-enforced structure where rights are upheld and respected. Second, the structure of that society must allow individuals to own themselves. And lastly, the structure must be such that individuals can have the opportunity and means to do what they want to do. Van Parijs's (1997: 6) makes these three principles clearer when he claims that a free society is one in which opportunities, 'access to the means for doing what one might want to do' are distributed so that 'some can have more opportunities than others, but only if their having more does not reduce the opportunities of those with less'. The egalitarian ideal of Van Parijs purports that institutions then must be designed to offer the greatest real opportunities to those with more limited means and limited opportunities, while still protecting formal freedoms.

Yet, the analysis of a free society as presented by Van Parijs goes further and becomes one where the moralization of freedom is at the centre of how he sees formal freedom and real freedom clashing. Van Parijs's outlines this by saying, 'libertarians have been led – sensibly – to giving a key role to property rights. But as a result of doing so, they have been misled – far less sensibly – into adopting an altogether implausible moralized conception of freedom … freedom is only restricted when my rights are violated' (Van Parijs, 1997: 16). Van Parijs outlines how libertarians have created this moralized construction of freedom and a resulting system where creating the right enforcements for property rights means total freedom for all, as if the power to own was a natural disposition, disconnected from social conditions. Instead, moralizing freedom creates an unequal allocation of freedoms and unfreedoms whereby while some might remain fully free to own property and do what they want with what they legitimately own, for example, many still remain unfree to fully and legitimately participate in the exercise of that right due to other social and structural constraints. Van Parijs's distinction between formal and real freedom wants to lay bare the inequalities that lie deep in societal and governmental arrangements, freedom as 'rights only' does not suffice his ideas about freedom, rather, freedom as participation and exercise of rights is closer to his real-freedom-for-all:

> This is why a libertarian had to call the island of our tale a free society, however despotic its owner's rule. Such counterintuitive implications clearly make the moralized conception of freedom untenable, and 'libertarianism' … and their alleged freedom-based case for capitalism, pure or otherwise a misleading label. Libertarians should rather be called rights-fetishists.
>
> *(Van Parijs, 1997: 16)*

These 'rights-fetishists', as Van Parijs calls them, uphold the purity of the value over and above the pragmatic way in which the value is played out in society. Universal basic income is an important part of how Van Parijs envisages a free society which respects real freedom. Van Parijs (1997) argues that if we are to truly discuss capitalism, we need to go beyond understanding capitalism as the private ownership of means of production, but also of capital. The capital that is produced in society is produced predominantly through waged labour, this dominance becomes problematic because private owners can decide what to do with their capital, while for the worker, their capital is their sustenance and they do not privately own the capital they produce. Think about how in society the majority of people work for a wage, their work is part of the owner's capital, tied to those who reap the benefits and accumulate capital. In contrast, the only thing you own is your salary, but this is also your sustenance, used to pay your way in society. For Van Parijs (1997: 7) these unequal relationships point to how in capitalist societies there are problems with 'self-ownership', 'like the ownership of the means of production, self-ownership is a matter of degree. Its scope varies depending on how large a proportion of a society's membership enjoys it, while its depth varies as a function of what each person is allowed to do with herself'. With this in mind, we are also owned by the private owners for whom we work and who own the capital produced through our labour. A universal basic income where everyone is paid a sum regardless of employment status, marital status or income generation, would help unravel the coercive relationship that capitalism produces because of its inevitable private ownership of means of production and capital, which includes the fruits of people's work.

A universal basic income would also help a free society protect people's real freedom. The emphasis on real freedom puts the emphasis on the means we need to attain the life we choose, thus the issue of a universal basic income becomes central to the idea of real-freedom-for-all. Van Parijs's real libertarianism is then proposed as the system of governance and administration which would implement such a regular payment, while also ensuring that everyone's formal freedom be protected. A universal basic income would be a recognition that we live in a form of capitalism that insidiously owns part of our freedom, even when we live in a system with formal freedoms. Capitalism also generates profits from our labour, and although we might get a wage, the private capital as a result of our work is not devolved to us, instead we gain our wage which further disenfranchises us. A universal basic income is perceived by Van Parijs as a step towards real-freedom-for-all, an important measure which will allow individuals to more truly own themselves.

Social justice and universal basic income

Social justice is integral to the idea of a universal basic income, since it refers to the fair distribution of wealth, privileges and social opportunities in society. A key theory to examine justice when debating universal basic income is John Rawls's (1999) *A Theory of Justice* (first published in 1971). Rawls, perhaps the most influential theorist to present a framework around the notion of social justice, provides a careful outline of how society and its institutions should be primarily concerned with social justice, with countering inequalities, but to do so in ways that still respect the chosen liberties upon which that society exists. Making sense of Rawls allows us to better understand how a universal basic income is socially just and the potential it has to address some of the issues around the unfair distribution of goods, income and wealth which characterize modern societies.

Rawlsian theory emphasizes how societies are marked by conflicts of interests since every society always upholds and validates certain positions over others, for example, the employed over the unemployed, or the healthy over the sick. Rawls (1999) refers to how the 'structure contains various social positions and that men born into different positions have different expectations of life determined, in part, by the political system as well as by economic and social circumstances' (Rawls, 1999: 7). These are inevitable and pervasive inequalities which are deeply rooted in every society and which cannot possibly be justified on the grounds of merit or talent. Rawls argues that it is these inequalities, present in the foundations of any society where social justice must begin. In order to make the case for social justice, Rawls discusses how in a society there is a need for developing what he calls principles of justice. Rawls explains some of these ideas when he claims:

> A set of principles is required for choosing among the various social arrangements which determine this division of advantages and for underwriting an agreement on the proper distributive shares. These principles are the principles of social justice: they provide a way of assigning rights and duties in the basic institutions of society and they define the appropriate distribution of the benefits and burdens of social cooperation.
>
> *(Rawls, 1999: 4)*

Rawls's (1999) theory consists of three principles which are ordered hierarchically. The *liberty principle* refers to a number of fundamental freedoms, such as the right to vote and the freedom of expression. But Rawls also lays out the *principle of fair equality of opportunity*, to prescribe how people with the same talents have equal access to all social positions. Lastly, under the constraints of the other two principles, Rawls lays out the *difference principle*, stipulating that the worst social position in society should be as high as possible.

Rawls defines this approach to social justice by introducing the concept of *maximin*; he asserts that 'the maximin rule tells us to rank alternatives by their worst possible outcomes: we are to adopt the alternative the worst outcome of which is superior to the worst outcomes of the others' (Rawls 1999: 133). With this principle applying to all social institutions Rawls is telling us that institutions should uphold the arrangement which will benefit those in the least advantaged positions. This is fundamental to how Rawls views social justice and how he describes the workings of social justice in society, through fundamentally just institutions which recognize and privilege the positions of those who are inherently disadvantaged. Van Parijs and Vanderborght (2017) point out that it is this last principle in particular, which provides justification for a universal basic income, as it does not only stipulate that there is a guaranteed minimum level of consumption, but also mentions 'wealth'.

A universal basic income bodes well with these ideas laid out, since Rawls also describes the importance of powers and prerogatives, and a universal basic income 'gives power to the weakest in both employment and household contexts' (Van Parijs and Vanderborght, 2017: 110). Furthermore, Rawls highlights his concern for the social bases of self-respect, which resonates with a universal basic income that can eradicate the stigmatization and humiliation that existing welfare policies possess. Rawls asserts that the principles of justice are needed since it is natural for people not to want to share equally the possible benefits and rewards a society can offer. Rawls describes this when he claims:

> persons are not indifferent as to how the greater benefits produced by their collaboration are distributed, for in order to pursue their ends they each prefer a larger to a lesser share. A set of principles is required … for underwriting an agreement on the proper distributive shares. These principles are the principles of social justice:

they provide a way of assigning rights and duties in the basic institutions of society and they define the appropriate distribution of the benefits and burdens of social cooperation.

(Rawls, 1999: 4)

For the principles of justice to be effective, Rawls (1999) says that we must operate behind a *veil of ignorance*. Rawls's veil of ignorance tells us that to live in a society means that there is an established set of institutional arrangements to live by in order to live a full life in that society. However, Rawls (1999) points out, that we do not know which position we might end up with. For instance, we know that to live in Western societies means that we are expected to be educated by going to school, to contribute to society financially by working and paying taxes, to find a sense of meaning and pride by being employed and productive, among others. We might turn out to be educated, employed and privileged in most institutional arrangements set by that society, or we might turn out to be, expelled from school, therefore unable to secure employment and disadvantaged in relation to the same predetermined institutional arrangements. Whichever way things go, we must be prepared to live the full life set out by that society and because we know that everyone's position will be different, a defined approach to social justice is needed.

The introduction of a universal basic income could help strike the right balance between those who are in the least advantaged positions and those who are in advantaged ones. A negative income tax is actually mentioned by Rawls as 'graded income supplement', provided to those who fall under a defined threshold and which should be guaranteed by the government, and given in the form of 'family allowances ... special payments for sickness and employment' (Rawls, 1999: 243). A universal basic income would go further and eliminate the associated stigma that is normally associated with means-tested government payments. A universal basic income also reduces the complexity and bureaucracy that precedes means-tested payments. The automatic and universal strategy would ensure that people do not lose out because of common problems with accessibility, for example, due to a lack of information, online procedures or other skills. The implementation of a universal basic income can help reach those people in society who fall through the net because they are in non-market activities, such as, out of continuous employment, affected by illness, or burdened by care responsibilities.

One of the main premises by Rawls, and one which helps understand how a basic income can be seen as an important factor for social justice is that of *primary goods*. Rawls refers to primary goods and natural goods, these goods are socially distributed and others are less dependent on society, yet, they are still influenced by society to a certain extent. Rawls is concerned with a just distribution of primary goods because they are the ones which are directly linked to the foundations of a society. Primary goods are understood to be what people need to be engaged in social cooperation and lead a full life as equal members of that society. Let's turn to Rawls for a more specific definition:

> the basic structure of society distributes certain primary goods, that is, things that every rational man is presumed to want. These goods normally have a use whatever a person's rational plan of life ... the chief primary goods at the disposition of society are rights, liberties, and opportunities, and income and wealth ... These are the social primary goods. Other primary goods such as health and vigor, intelligence and imagination, are natural goods; although their possession is influenced by the basic structure, they are not so directly under its control. Imagine, then, a hypothetical initial arrangement in which all the social primary goods are equally distributed: everyone has similar rights and duties, and income and wealth are evenly shared.
>
> *(Rawls, 1999: 54)*

A universal basic income would satisfy Rawls's argument of how primary goods need to be fairly distributed in any society with socially just institutions. The usual problems around whether everyone is deserving of a universal basic income, particularly those who choose not to work, or those who work in non-remunerated activities, such as care or volunteering work, dissipate as a universal basic income distributes wealth without the limitations of means-tested payments.

Rawls also offers another basis upon which a universal basic income might prove beneficial to society. This is based on the inclusion of self-respect as a primary good – Rawls says of the distribution of primary goods, that 'all social values – liberty and opportunity, income and wealth, and the social bases of self-respect – are to be distributed equally' (Rawls, 1999: 54). Rawls considered self-respect as one of the most important primary goods, as it allows us to find meaning in what we do and be willing to participate in society. Rawls explained these ideas further:

> men's self-respect ... increases the effectiveness of social coopera-
> tion ... It is clearly rational for men to secure their self-respect. A
> sense of their own worth is necessary if they are to pursue their
> conception of the good with satisfaction and to take pleasure in its
> fulfillment. Self-respect is not so much a part of any rational plan
> of life as the sense that one's plan is worth carrying out ...
>
> *(Rawls, 1999: 155)*

A universal basic income can create the social disposition which recognizes the different positions people occupy in a society and how societies inevitably produce inequalities. Hence, as Rawls's arguments show, a universal strategy is needed to uphold social justice. Social justice according to Rawls involves recognizing that society influences the lives of individuals in many ways which are difficult to estimate. In Rawls's view society affects both primary goods and natural goods, and all individuals will occupy different positions which are sometimes privileged and sometimes less so. However, the state and its institutions have more control over primary goods as they are the ones which can be addressed through society's main institutions, for example, if we want individuals to be educated, we invest more in education and schooling. Similarly, if we want to support the distribution of these primary goods, including the notion of self-respect, a universal basic income can help lay a uniform foundation for social justice.

Summary

Exploring the notion of a universal basic income implies that we understand how basic values, such as equality, freedom and social justice, need further reflection. In modern societies which grow increasingly unequal and where new inequalities are emerging everyday there is a need to rethink how we construct the basis for social injustice to continue. For instance, by opening up the broader notion of work, and not just labour sold to an employer, we can challenge poor structural arrangements in the societies we live. A universal basic income can contribute to ameliorate such conditions of work and employment that are becoming more prevalent, while creating a new basis of social justice which is not so focused on what individuals can do for themselves, but what a fairer distribution of income can do for society. Following various theorists, this chapter has discussed the potential a universal basic income can have on the continuity of important values, such as freedom, social justice and equality.

Marxist perspectives can be used to harness the potential a universal basic income has to increase workers' power in the face of employers who might be reducing employee's rights for the sake of profit. Also, a universal basic income can help broaden the notion of work in society and recognize with regular payments the unrecognized work that is carried out by many people in the form of care, child rearing and volunteering. A universal basic income can also open up more freedoms and the exercise of rights for those people in society who are disadvantaged by lack of income. In terms of social justice this chapter has also endeavoured to discuss how a universal basic income can level the inevitable inequalities that living in a society can bring.

This chapter has also explored the notion of freedom as described by Van Parijs (1997). Van Parijs argues that real freedom is entangled with social justice, this means not just thinking of freedom as an abstract value, but instead as a practical pursuit, namely, what can we really do in a free society? How might we be limited by lack of means and resources? Van Parijs purports that there less value in thinking about all the possibilities living in a free society offers, if there are large sections of the population who are systematically kept away from these possibilities due to lack of means. This chapter presented how Van Parijs criticizes how freedom has been thought about as just a value or an aspiration, and instead claims that real-freedom-for all is about people actually being able to take up an opportunity and obtain a valuable outcome from it, not just having an equal opportunity to access it. For Van Parijs then the focus on freedom should be on striving for an egalitarian approach by institutions whose efforts should diminish the barriers that society naturally imposes on individuals.

Lastly, the chapter also looked into Rawls's theories of social justice and how a universal basic income might help satisfy Rawls's claim that a just society is one where there is an equal distribution of primary goods. The chapter picked the distribution of goods as an essential part of how social justice happens in society because although there are some natural goods which are less influenced by society, there are many other primary goods which are heavily influenced by our social environment, such as, wealth, work and education. When discussing Rawls, the chapter paid some attention to how Rawls included the notion of self-respect in his primary goods. The chapter also critically examined how if self-respect is a primary good in society, what the role of a universal basic income could be. Social justice was discussed as an important foundation of all social institutions and that if social institutions are to remain just, then they must participate in a fair distribution of goods in society, regardless of whether these goods are abstract or pragmatic.

The idea of a universal basic income sheds a different light on all of these historical and theoretical debates. How societies create pathways for equality, freedom and social justice will naturally change if a universal basic income came into full implementation and this chapter has had two main purposes. Firstly, it has introduced some key debates and secondly, it has critically explored some implications around equality, freedom and social justice that could be debated with the introduction of a universal basic income.

References

Atkinson, A. B. (2015) *Inequality: What Can Be Done?* Cambridge, MA: Harvard University Press.

Bellofiore, R. (2009) *Rosa Luxembourg and the Critique of Political Economy*. London: Routledge.

Clark, D. (2002) 'The World Bank and human rights: The need for greater accountability'. *Harvard Human Rights Journal*, 15(1), pp. 205–226.

Dahms, H. (2015) 'Which capital, which Marx? Basic income between mainstream economics, critical theory and the logic of capital'. *Basic Income*

Studies, 10(1), pp. 115–140. Gorz, A. (1999) *Reclaiming Work: Beyond a Wage-Based Society*. Cambridge: Cambridge Policy Press.

Harrop, A. and Tait, C. (2017) *Universal Basic Income and the Future of Work*. London: Fabian Society.

Manjarin, E. and Szlinder, M. (2016) 'A Marxist argumentative scheme on basic income and wage share in an anti-capitalist agenda'. *Basic Income Studies* 11 (1), pp. 49–59.

Marx, K. (2007) *Economic and Philosophic Manuscripts of 1844*. New York: Dover Publications.

McDonough, B. (2017) 'Precarious work and unemployment in Europe'. In: S. Isaacs, ed. *European Social Problems*. London: Routledge.

OECD. (1996) *The Knowledge Based Economy*. Paris: OECD.

Piketty, T. (2014) *Capital in the Twenty-first Century*. Cambridge, MA: Belknap Press.

Pitts, F. H., Lombardozzi, L. and Warner, N. (2017) 'Speenhamland, automation and the basic income: A warning from history?' *Renewal: A Journal of Labour Politics*, 25(3), pp. 145–155.

Rawls, J. (1999) *A Theory of Justice*. Cambridge, MA: Belknap Press.

Standing, G. (2015) *The Precariat: A New Dangerous Class*. London: Penguin.

Standing, G. (2017) *Basic Income: And How We Can Make It Happen*. London: Penguin.

Švarc, J. and Dabić, M. (2017) 'Evolution of the knowledge economy: A historical perspective with an application to the case of Europe'. *Journal of the Knowledge Economy*, 8, pp. 159–176.

Van Parijs, P. (1997) *Real Freedom for All: What (if anything) Can Justify Capitalism?* Oxford: Clarendon Press.

Van Parijs, P. (2003) 'A basic income for all'. In: P. Van Parijs, J. Cohen and J. Rogers, eds. *What's Wrong with a Free Lunch?* London: Beacon Press.

Van Parijs, P. and Vanderborght, Y. (2017) *Basic Income: A Radical Proposal for a free Society and a Sane Economy*. Cambridge, MA: Harvard University Press. Wilczyńska, A., Batorski, D. and Torrent-Sellens, J. (2018) 'Precarious knowledge work? The combined effect of occupational unemployment and flexible employment on job insecurity'. *Journal of the Knowledge Economy*, 11 (6), pp. 1–24.

3

ADDRESSING PRECARIOUS WORK AND SOCIAL INEQUALITIES

What a universal basic income can do

Introduction

Against the backdrop of Guy Standing's (2015a) work *The Precariat: A New Dangerous Class* and other contemporary perspectives that lay foundations for a universal income, this chapter discusses universal basic income in relation to precarious work and social inequalities. It describes the inequalities experienced by those who suffer from the economic effects of neoliberalism – precarious workers who are subject to insecure, unprotected and poorly paid working conditions. Drawing on Uber, 'McJobs' and other contemporary examples, this chapter maps out how a universal basic income can remedy some of the problems of precarious and insecure forms of employment and livelihood. Drawing on Standing (2015a), this chapter examines how a universal basic income might address insecurity – a key feature of modern capitalist life. It also addresses the role of technology and automation, the reluctance to recruit people (Stern, 2016) and an analysis of what Brynjolfsson and McAfee (2016) call the 'Second Machine Age'. By examining the knock-on effects of precarious work in particular, this chapter shows how a universal basic income can rescue some of the shortcomings of the digital age, providing a safety net for the gig economy, allowing people more flexibility in relation to work and helping to provide them with more balanced lifestyles.

Re-conceptualizing 'work'

Universal basic income cannot be fully understood unless we question the significance and role that 'work' and 'employment' play in society. In most societies, work occupies a large part of an individual's life. Most people work to earn a living, or they rely on pensions and other benefits collected from taxes which other employed people have contributed towards. In common-sense or lay terms, we usually define 'work' as task-based activities for which people are paid by an employer, customer or client. However, this un-sociological and common-sense definition of 'work' fails to recognize the huge amounts of 'work' which goes unpaid. For example, 'care workers' who are employed for an organization get a 'real wage', whereas those 'carers' who look after children, partners, or elderly relatives usually do not get paid at all. And despite the nature of the work being exactly the same in many cases, the social status of paid carers and unpaid carers is completely different, with the former having more recognition, as well as having all the benefits which employment can bring (for example: holidays, sick pay and pensions). In the UK, for example, the Office for National Statistics (ONS) reported that some 5.8 million people were providing unpaid care in England and Wales in 2011. Carers aren't the only people who are unpaid in many societies. Many community workers, unpaid charity fundraisers, and 'work experience' employees are also essentially 'working for free'. Doing 'real' work, it seems, means earning a wage. This conception of work is nothing new. In the 1980s, the British prime minister Margaret Thatcher told the people of the UK that the Victorian work ethic must be revived and people must 'do an honest day's work for an honest day's pay'. The 'work ethic', as it is known, makes people believe that they ought to work, whether they need to or not. In Britain especially, where the notion of 'work ethic' is most prominent, non-workers are seen as less valuable to society than those who put in 'a hard days graft'. The 'work ethic' is of course a discourse which permeates in every corner of industrialized society. And yet in most industrialized societies, more than half of the population are either, too old, too young, too sick or too rich to work. The very idea that everyone works or somehow must work is itself a fictitious narrative driven by a neoliberal discourse which is preoccupied with the importance of paid employment and the idea of 'inclusion in the labour market' (Levitas, 2005). As the nineteenth-century sociologist Max Weber (1864–1920) pointed out, the idea that work in itself constitutes a value has its historical origin in particular parts of Europe following the period of the Reformation and extending into the eighteenth century (McDonough, 2015). The consequence is that neoliberal culture polarizes the notion of the 'work ethic' with 'idleness' and even 'contempt'. The philosophy and discourse of a universal basic income, in contrast, does not set up a division between the employed and non-employed. On the contrary, it provides a more egalitarian and liberal discourse, which understands individuals as valued citizens of our society whether they work in employment or not.

Gorz (1999) re-conceptualizes work and abandons the work ethic altogether (see also Chapter 2). Pressing for a universal basic income, he says that: 'it has to be recognized that neither the right to an income, nor full citizenship, nor everyone's sense of identity and self-fulfilment can any longer be centred on and depend on occupying a job' (Gorz, 1999: 54). Drawing on Gorz and other Marxist thinkers, a universal basic income has the potential to take us beyond a wage-based society and allow for a system where there is no longer an exploitation of the wage relation. Gorz (1999) argues for a universal basic income which is both unconditional and adequate for a decent existence in society. Rather than having the flexibility *of* workers, Gorz (1999) argues for the flexibility *for* workers. On these terms, he believes that there can be an effective validation and adequate recompense for, caring, voluntary and non-market activities. A universal basic income, combined with good public services and ecologically sustainable urban regeneration would provide genuine inclusion and greater equality.

Work then, must be re-conceptualized to define a much wider range of human activities in which we engage in, which help to maintain modern capitalist society. Many tasks we are involved in, and 'work' we do, keeps afloat capitalist society even if it does *not* require 'earning a wage' or having a contract of employment – like being a mother and raising children. However, in an era where permanent contracts of employment are becoming less sought after and precarious jobs are becoming increasingly more common, even paid employment does not 'earn an honest day's pay' (as Thatcher had once argued).

Precarious work and the call for a universal basic income

What is precarious work? Precarious work refers to insecure, non-standard work, with unprotected and poor quality work conditions. In recent years there has been a dramatic increase in precarious work, owing to globalization and changes to the economy. In particular, there has been a shift from manufacturing work to service sector work, a proliferation in the use of new technologies, and a demand for more flexibility in the workplace. As a result, there has been a decline in standard employment contracts and widespread use of short-term, 'zero-hour' contracts with exploitative working conditions and a lack of fringe benefits for employees. The rise in precarious work has created political, economic and policy debates all over the world. In Germany, for example, there has been fierce political debate on the *Erosion der Normalarbeitsverhältnisse*, that is, the erosion of collectively regulated employment. While in France, there has been much discussion around the idea of *statut* or 'status', referring to the social identity, personal security and sense of worth a job brings with it in contemporary French society. In Spain, there are widespread discussions focussed on *precariedad laboral*, that is, precarious labour, or on *trabajo temporal* (temporary employment). In many countries, such as Britain and the US, there are growing concerns that precarious work is part of an increasing gap between the richest and poorest in society. Workforces are increasingly divided between insecure, low-skilled, low-paid work, with higher-paid, higher-skilled and properly contracted employment.

One example to note is the global taxi company Uber, which uses technology as an easy way to reach out towards customers in several countries across the world – providing a means by which users can find quick, cheap and accessible transport at the click of a button. But the technology is also used to recruit taxi drivers, who are required to drive customers around at cheap prices, enabling Uber to be a global leader in transport. The problem is that 'Uber's multinational approach has been driven by a neoliberalist tendency to accelerate privatization, promote deregulation and to operate with minimalist interference from the state' (McDonough, 2017: 100). As a result, companies like Uber try to avoid government regulation, with workers suffering from the consequences. Uber workers are supposedly 'self-employed'. However, they lack most of the benefits of self-employed people, such as control over their client or customer base and the setting of their own charges and prices. In reality, of course, Uber workers should be given permanent contracts of employment, so they can have the right for employers to pay for social security, disability and unemployment insurance, the right to sick pay; the right to take holiday, the right to have maternity or paternity paid leave, retirement benefits, and the right to create or be part of an organized trade union. In October 2017, Uber drivers in the UK won a legal battle for workers' rights, entitling them to the minimum wage and holiday pay. Judge Anthony Snelson, who led the tribunal panel, was critical of Uber's claim that its drivers are 'self-employed', stating that 'The notion that Uber in London is a mosaic of 30,000 small businesses linked by a common "platform" is to our minds faintly ridiculous' (Booth, 2016). The legal decision will impact upon thousands of Uber drivers in Britain, as well as thousands of others working in what is known as the 'gig economy' whose employers wrongly classify them as self-employed and deny them the rights to which they are duly entitled to by law.

The 'gig economy' is characterized by an unstable and insecure environment which renders people and their labour as commodities to be bought, sold and bargained with. Standing's (2015a) *The Precariat: The New Dangerous Class*, provides an account of an emerging class of people, whom facing insecurity are continually moving in and out of precarious work. Standing (2015a) shows how precarious employment is a consequence of neoliberal economics. In the pursuit of market efficiency, the labour markets of economies are opened up through deregulation and everything becomes commodified. Standing (2015a: 44) explains that we treat 'everything as a commodity to be bought and sold, subject to market forces, with prices set by demand and supply, without effective 'agency' (a capacity to resist)' (Standing 2015a: 44). Commodification makes the division of labour within organizations more fluid. If work activities can be carried out more cheaply in one location than another, they can be 'offshored (within firms) or "outsourced"' (to partner firms or others)' (Standing 2015a: 51). Standing (2015a) argues that this fragments the labour process since internal job structures and 'careers' are disrupted due to uncertainty over whether jobs people might have expected to do will be offshored or outsourced. But precarious work should not be understood as something which is inevitable and unstoppable. On the contrary, precarious work is a result of the sorts of economics governments willingly adopt. And poor and unstable work conditions can be exacerbated by government policies and employment law.

To describe precarious work, some scholars have also used the term 'McJobs' to describe the casual, low wage and low-prestige jobs carried out across various sectors. Coined by a sociologist in an article in *The Washington Post* (US) entitled: 'The Fast-Food Factories: McJobs are Bad for Kids', author Etzioni (1986) argued that McJobs (jobs in fast food outlets such as McDonalds) were highly routinized and so tightly controlled by management that the roles gave employees little autonomy or creative freedom to develop their personal skills. In a more recent study of the McDonalds fast-food chain in Australia, Gould (2010) found that employees view their jobs as repeatedly doing a limited range of non-complex tasks. However, he also found that fast-food work does offer some human resource advantages, potential career opportunities and for some, desirable forms of work organization. McJobs, however, are usually perceived as some of the worst forms of labour in contemporary societies in the developed world. Likened to factory work, McJobs are usually repetitive, low-skilled and quite often poorly paid. And if workers do not live up to the expectations of the organization, they can easily be 'let go' or replaced.

There are currently some misconceptions of precarious work. First, precarious work does not only affect Uber drivers, fast-food workers, and other working-class occupations. On the contrary, precarious employment affects university lecturers (many on zero-hour contracts), doctors and nurses (on unrealistic shift patterns and pay conditions) and a wide-range of other middle-class occupations. Second, precarious work doesn't just affect the workers themselves, but also customers, clients and service users. In a study of precarious work in hospitals across Europe, for example, Rotenberg et al. (2008) found that the adverse effects of job insecurity can be harmful to health for both patients and workers. Workers with insecure and poor working conditions in hospitals are less likely to be able to dedicate themselves to patients, are more likely to be under-skilled and inexperienced, and are often asked to commit themselves to tasks which they are not trained or paid adequately to carry out. Drawing on this evidence, precarious working conditions are as poor for the customers and users of services as they are for the workers themselves.

In response to the problem of precarious work, political parties, human rights and community activists and academics from countries around the globe are calling for a universal basic income scheme which can help to minimize the devastating impact that precarious work can have on individuals, families and communities across society. Long gone is the traditional way of obtaining work – moving into a career ones father or family once did. On the contrary, today's workers must be multi-skilled and multi-talented, willing to move from one precarious job to the next – depending on what the market forces call for. Universal basic income provides a safety net for this new market economy and provides stability in an era where instability reigns.

Standing adds that a universal basic income would be the most effective way of reducing poverty because it can overcome 'poverty traps' and would reduce 'precarity traps' (Standing, 2017: 76–77). 'Poverty traps' refer to situations in which increases in income are offset by a consequent loss of state benefits. For example, someone living on low state benefits find that they are no better off financially when finding work in a low paid job. A universal basic income, in contrast to means-tested benefits, is given to everyone regardless of whether or not they work. When unemployed people move into work, they immediately benefit from the pay they receive from their employment – they are financially better-off. A universal basic income can also reduce 'precarity traps' – situations in which delays in paying means-tested benefits act as a 'disincentive to take short-term or casual jobs' (Standing, 2017: 77). Because of the complexity and bureaucracy of modern welfare systems, people entitled to means-tested and conditional benefits often have to wait to receive benefit payments. This was typically the case with the rollout of Britain's Universal Credit in 2018, a welfare plan which resulted in long delays (sometimes up to six weeks) in recipients receiving benefits. These delays create periods of debt and poverty, and discourage people from applying for casual, short-term, low-paying jobs they may otherwise be interested in. But with the fear of losing benefit entitlements and having to start all over again in applying for them (should the job not work out), the bureaucracy and form-filling efforts required act as a deterrent and puts people off moving into work. This 'precarity trap', as Standing calls it, could be reduced with the introduction of a universal basic income. With a steady income stream, people are not put off from trying out new occupations, on short-term or long-term contracts of employment. Standing (2017) argues that a basic income paid as a *right* would help to avoid the 'poverty trap' and 'precarity trap' – it would reduce the moral hazard which ensues from existing social assistance schemes in most industrialized countries, because it would free up and allow people to do what they really want – to get a job. Far from discouraging work, as some critics have argued, Standing (2017) provides good arguments to show that a universal basic income would incentivize people to work in many respects.

How can a universal basic income tackle social inequalities and increase opportunities?

Many argue that a universal basic income has the potential to tackle social inequalities and provide new financial and social opportunities. One of the most controversial debates regarding universal basic income is whether giving income to every member of society is the best solution for dealing with social inequalities. At first sight, it seems obvious that welfare policies which wish to tackle social inequality, should focus on providing for those suffering worst from social inequality – by giving basic income only to the poor, for example. However, regardless of how counterintuitive it might seem, giving a basic income to all is far more likely to bring about social equality. Torry provides a good explanation of this, discussing how a universal basic income can work in developed countries, illustrating why it should be a universal policy:

> To give money only to the poor requires us to take that money away as soon as someone ceases to be poor. So a poor person who finds a job, or who increases their initially low income, finds their

benefits being reduced, and they might at the same time find themselves paying income tax, other deductions, and fares to work: so they remain poor. The answer to this difficulty would appear to be to allow them to keep their benefits for a while: but that would set up an injustice, because someone who had not been on those benefits, and was on the same wages, would be worse off than the person who had been on benefits and had been allowed to keep them. The only answer is to give money to everyone, and to allow everyone to keep it, whatever happens to their earnings.

(Torry, 2016: 45)

Torry (2016) explains that a monetary system of income which is universal can help to bring about social equality. But it is not just monetary income itself which is most important. Standing (2015a) argues that the emancipatory value of a universal basic income is greater than the monetary value. Drawing on the results of a large-scale basic income scheme conducted in the Indian State of Madhya Pradesh between 2010 and 2013 (described in Chapter 4), Standing (2015a) argues that a basic income improves economic security beyond its monetary value. For Standing (2017), a universal basic income provides economic security, which counteracts the insecurity experienced in many communities. But what is 'insecurity'? Standing (2015b) says that insecurity arises from the combination of four key things: risk, hazards, shocks and uncertainty. First, Standing (2015b) distinguishes between *entrepreneurial risk* and *dependency risk*. Entrepreneurial risk arises from attempts to increase income or production while dependency risk arises from borrowing to acquire an asset. Drawing on the study in Madhya Pradesh, India, Standing (2015b) argues that dependency risk is impoverishing and often leads to debt bondage. In the Indian villages where Standing (2015b) researched, borrowers were locked into 'quasi-permanent debt relationships dominated by the lender, who can determine when, where, and how much labour will be performed, and what the wage will be' (Standing, 2015b: 198). Because in Madhya Pradesh labour is seasonal, and at harvest time the market wage is well above its level in the slack season, so it is that landlords choose to use debt to obtain labour for the harvest, always below the market wage. But insecurity also arises from *hazards*. A hazard is a life-cycle event that in it-self may be desired but which is costly, such as a marriage, birth of a child, or

family celebration. These are major events which culturally institutionalized and create high costs. A *shock* also contributes to insecurity. A shock is
'an event that hits or affects whole communities or households' (Standing,
2015b: 199). Typical shocks in developing nations are droughts, floods,
earthquakes or harvest failure. These too are costly and can in some cases
destroy whole livelihoods in one hit. Finally, insecurity also arises from
uncertainty. Standing (2015b: 199) describes this as 'unknown unknowns',
for which it is not possible to calculate the probability of an adverse event.
In short, Standing (2015b) argues that a universal basic income can reduce
insecurity, in other words it can reduce risk, hazards, shock and uncertainty. A key point which Standing (2017) makes, is that universal basic
income is more than just money given to communities. Standing (2015b:
199) argues that a universal basic income can provide a *basic security* which
can 'increase entrepreneurial risk-taking, because it would help assure the
means to cope, and the means to recover, should the venture fail'. But a
universal basic income would also reduce 'dependency risk-taking' by
reducing the need to borrow. Standing (2015b) believes that a universal
basic income would strengthen personal, family and community resilience,
since fragility is associated with income insecurity. Standing (2015b) also
argues that a scarcity of commodities can shorten people's planning horizons, block out the consideration of some options, and produce chronic
anxiety. In other words, those who sense a scarcity of money, or of time
and food, are prone to suffer from a 'scarcity mind-set' (Standing, 2015b:
197). The scarcity of commodities shapes behaviour and attitudes which
curtails people's opportunities to escape poverty. People with a scarcity
mind-set are less likely to take forward new initiatives or to take entrepreneurial risks. A universal basic income has the potential to break the
scarcity mind-set and offer opportunities for individuals and families to
invest in their futures.

Technological unemployment and the impact of new technologies on workers

The potential threat of technological unemployment has long been
debated in boardrooms and by trade union officers, but it is an important issue among social policy-makers too. A key issue is whether or
not predictions about large scale job losses will materialize and how the

state and the labour market will respond to such changes. Generally, 'technological unemployment' refers to the loss of jobs caused by technological change and is a real threat to the working lives of large amounts of people in many societies around the world. As a consequence, some argue that the state requires a welfare policy (such as universal basic income) which compensates for the growth of technological unemployment.

The idea that technology can have adverse effects on people's work has been around for a very long time. Since the industrial revolution of the eighteenth century, the introduction of technology has had varying effects on employment. In the early nineteenth century, for example, Luddites – bands of English workers in various industrial sectors of work (such as cotton and woollen mills) – would break and destroy machinery to protest against the adverse effects technology was having on standard labour practices. Over two hundreds later, technology is still having a profound impact on the lives of many in employment. Technological innovations have seen many jobs decline over the last thirty years. One example is the emergence of the internet and the PC (personal computer) in the 1980s which saw the insurance industry shrink, in terms of workers doing or associated with insurance underwriting. Another example is the replacement of car factory plant workers with robots – as described in Beynon's (1973) classic text *Working for Ford* – which resulted in the alienation of workers (an estrangement and unfulfilment with the tasks workers are directly involved with). Since the 1970s and 1980s, technology continues to have a profound effect on the car industry – more recently the emergence of CAD (computer-aided design) has revolutionized the car design industry – reducing mass numbers of designers needed to carry out tasks which could now be done by a computer program. Today, computer software is now also replacing journalists by automatically crawling through the worldwide web and synthesizing news items electronically. Even traders in financial markets are being replaced by automated algorithms. By eliminating certain tasks and deskilling many jobs, technology can, in many ways, be seen as detrimental to the lives of people in numerous sectors or industries.

The notion of de-skilling was central to Braverman's (1998) work called *Labour and Monopoly Capitalism: The Degradation of Work in the Twentieth*

Century (first published in 1974). Braverman (1998) argues that the des-killing effect occurs when skilled labour is replaced by automation (which can be operated by less skilled labour). Braverman (1998) shows how managerial strategies are used to increase production and improve economic efficiency but have adverse effects on workers. Among other things, Braverman's (1998) work showed how *Taylorism* was contributing towards the degradation of work in the twentieth century. Taylorism refers to the scientific management often used in mass production, and owes its name to Frederick Taylor, who wrote *The Principles of Scientific Management* in 1911. Taylor (2011) was an American engineer and later became a management consultant on how to improve industrial efficiency. He was a proponent of the idea of scientific management when describing how best to maximize the potential of manufacturing industries (such as the production of steel). Braverman (1998) shows how workers were reduced to objects, rationally moved around, replaced and/or deskilled at the will of management. But Braverman (1998), drawing on Marxism, pointed out that it was not technology which cut jobs – but capitalist forms of management –operating within a capitalist system of property relations in which a large majority worked and a tiny minority owned or administered capital.

Braverman's (1998) work is as relevant today in showing how workers are increasingly over-worked, deskilled and made technologically unemployed in an ever changing and precarious economic environment. It is for some of these reasons why a universal basic income has been piloted and experimented with, in various countries all over the world (see Chapter 4 on universal basic income pilots and experiments). The scientific management of people within work organizations and the constant strive to become ever more productive puts technology at the heart of decision making. The question arises on what to do with people if society's needs can be met through the use of automated technologies and processes.

Automation and the rise of the machines: changing the nature of work

The developments of new low cost technologies has meant increased use of them at work and elsewhere, giving rise to automated processes wherever possible. Automation and increased use of technology has the potential to see an end to many people's jobs across a range of industries, and at a very minimum, changes the nature of work. It is for these reasons why automation and technology is tied to the idea of a universal basic income. The speed at which these new technologies are developing has questioned how people will find work if more and more jobs are replaced with technology. Replacing humans can mean anything from factory production lines (consider the expansion of machinery in Ford factories from 1960s to present day), to self-serving machines in supermarkets (and the consequent reduction of frontline staff). The replacement of humans can take place from using basic automation, to the use of expert systems, through to fully developed AI (artificial intelligence). The expansion of modern AI is bringing to life what has only ever been witnessed in fiction. For example, in 2017, driverless cars on sale by Nissan (and other car manufacturers) make AI not a far-fetched thing of the future, but a thing of the present. Even Uber (as discussed earlier) have outlined the creation of driverless taxis. After all, we already have widely used auto-pilot systems on board commercial aeroplanes as well as drones (unmanned aerial vehicles) for military and government operations. These developments led a leading physicist, the late Professor Stephen Hawking, to argue that AI could 'spell the end of the human race' (quoted on BBC News, 2 December 2014). With these perspectives in mind, the need for governments around the world to take stock of these changes, and develop policies to protect the livelihoods of people seems appropriate. When car manufacturers like Ford and Mercedes-Benz put forward proposals to develop self-driving taxis, it is governments who must respond with how society might cope with the losses of taxi drivers on the streets of its cities.

There are several other examples of how technology is impacting upon the jobs of people. In his work entitled *Raising the Floor: How a Universal Basic Income Can Renew Our Economy and Rebuild Our American Dream*, author Andy Stern (2016) provides an array of examples of automation taking over jobs within the US economy. For instance, in the farming and dairy industries of industrialized countries, milking cows was once hands-on work, with farm labourers milking cows one by one. But today a range of technologies are used to milk cows. Computers chart each cow's 'milking speed' and lasers are used to scan their underbellies, lining up for automated milking five or six times a day, 'monitoring the amount and quality of the milk they produce' (Stern, 2016: 56). In medicine and healthcare, IBM's Watson is developing 'the world's foremost diagnostician of cancer-related ailments' (Stern, 2016: 57). Watson is being programmed to sift through and keep up to date with the latest high quality published medical information, matching patients' symptoms and medical histories to formulate a diagnosis and treatment plan. In the UK, Babylon, an artificial intelligence medical start up based in Kensington, London, has created a controversial app called GP at Hand where patients type symptoms into a purple interface and a 'chatbot' types back, attempting to diagnose patients. But that's not all. Lowes, an American company that operates a chain of retail home improvement and appliance stores in the United States, has introduced a new autonomous in-store robot called 'NAVii'. The 'LoweBot' speaks multiple languages, and has been deployed in several stores to help guide home improvers around the store in order to locate items. Another example is Knightscope, a Silicon Valley start-up, which has introduced a five-foot tall robotic guard that can roam a retail store or office building searching for intruders during the night (Stern, 2016). On a cruise ship called *Quantum of the Seas*, a robotic bartender will begin serving a variety of customized drinks (Stern, 2016). Not only might it see some bartenders out of a job on the ship, but it might also be implemented in US city bars, creating an infinite supply of 'labour' that requires no wage, no lunch break, and requires no time off for holidays. A technologically driven society is one which puts people on the back burner, automates processes wherever possible, and replaces the need for 'real' workers whenever and wherever it can. It is for these reasons why the growth in automation and AI has been linked to a growing debate about universal basic income. In an age in which businesses look to replace people with new technologies, the call for an economic safety net becomes more and more urgent.

The impact of technology on jobs and call for a universal basic income

For many years there has been an assumption that new technologies 'boost economic productivity, lower the costs of production, and increase the supply of cheap goods, which, in turn, stimulates purchasing power, expands markets, and generates more jobs' (Rifkin, 1995: 15). This assumption has been the foundation for every industrial nation in the world. In *The End of Work*, Jeremy Rifkin argues that this logic has led to 'unprecedented levels of technological unemployment' and 'a precipitous decline in purchasing power' (Rifkin, 1995: 15). Rifkin says that the idea that benefits brought on by advances in technology and improvements in productivity eventually filter down to mass workers in terms of cheaper goods, greater purchasing power, and more jobs is a theory of 'trickle-down technology' (Rifkin, 1995: 15). Drawing on this metaphor, is the idea everyone benefits from the trickle-down effect of new technologies, from businesses to workers and consumers. Unfortunately, the promise that new technologies will bring prosperity, fails to live up to expectations. Technologies aren't created with the purpose of giving people other work to do. The point exercised by most businesses in the twenty-first century is to do away with labour costs altogether, or at least wherever is possible. Any business owner knows that hiring people comes with costs and a range of issues which is a consequence of managing people.

Stern (2016) shows how technology is impacting upon US jobs, through new technologies and automation, arguing that bold new policies are needed to reduce income inequality and prevent further diminishment of 'the American Dream'. An investment banker who worked in Silicon Valley and Wall Street said: 'Assume technology will replace every single job that exists … The question is, what do we decide to do with people?' (Stern, 2016: 60–61). Stern (2016: 65) argues that for the most part, 'automation is good and inevitable'. But he also says that 'unless significantly more work or new types of jobs are created, increased automation will result in the loss of more cherished middle-income jobs causing considerable pain in too many middle- and lower-income American families' (Stern, 2016: 65). One of the fundamental reasons for developing a universal basic income is to provide a safety net for people. But businesses which are driven by neoliberal economics have simply had enough of people, choosing to dispose of them wherever possible. Stern (2016) explains why replacing people with new technologies are an unfortunate but inevitable part of business development. Stern quotes an investment banker who oversees the employment of people in a large commercial bank:

If I hire someone, I've got to train them, manage them, and fire them. I've got to worry about them getting sick, their kids and dog getting sick. If a woman gets pregnant and goes on maternity leave for three months, I have to figure out how to cover for her. She might feel discriminated against, or harassed. People want to know where they stand: to get a performance review at the end of the year and eventually a promotion. I have to work out health benefits, severance, and vacation schedules for them. It goes on and on and on.

(Stern, 2016: 67–68)

The reality is that firms do not want 'the headache' involved with managing and dealing with people. Businesses want to do away with these problems by laying-off people and investing in systems which can manage cost centres, automate billings, and carryout all manufacturing that is required. Also, there is a huge list of problems which people can bring: 'Rogue traders, foreign bribes, discrimination and harassment, violence in the workplace – the list goes on' (Stern, 2016: 68). Stern (2016: 70) believes that there are entrepreneurs and venture capitalists reaping the benefits and 'techno-dancing to the tune' of more efficiency and productivity, which will mean fewer jobs. While 'robots and AI won't replace every worker, they'll make workers far more productive and cut down on the total number needed to do the work' (Stern, 2016: 70). At the same time new technologies make it easier for companies to hire contract workers instead of full-time employees (Stern, 2016), thus proliferating precarious work (see previous sections on precarious work).

In *The Second Machine Age: Work Progress, and Prosperity in a Time of Brilliant Technologies* Brynjolfsson and McAfee (2016) argue that we are living in a time of astonishing progress with digital technologies. As computers become more powerful 'companies have less need for some kinds of workers' (Brynjolfsson and McAfee, 2016: 10). Technological progress is going to leave behind a lot of people:

there's never been a better time to be a worker with special skills or the right education, because these people can use technology to create and capture value. However, there's never been a worse time to be a worker with only 'ordinary' skills and abilities to offer, because computers, robots, and other digital technologies are acquiring these skills and abilities at an extraordinary rate.

(Brynjolfsson and McAfee, 2016: 10)

Brynjolfsson and McAfee (2016) describe the progress of the second machine age by *bounty* and *spread*. Bounty refers to the 'increase in volume, variety, and quality and the decrease in cost of the many offerings brought on by modern technological progress' (Brynjolfsson and McAfee, 2016: 11). Spread, however, refers to the 'even-bigger differences among people in economic success – wealth, income, mobility, and other important measures' (Brynjolfsson and McAfee, 2016: 11). They say that spread has been increasing in recent years arguing that this is a troubling development which requires intervention. Ideally, they want to maximize the bounty while mitigating the negative effects of the spread (Brynjolfsson and McAfee, 2016).

One example Brynjolfsson and McAfee (2016) describe is the history of photography. Because of the profound effects of the digital age, it has been estimated that more photos are taken today every two minutes than in all of the nineteenth century (Brynjolfsson and McAfee, 2016). We now 'record the people and events of our lives with unprecedented detail and frequency, and share them more widely and easily than ever before' (Brynjolfsson and McAfee, 2016: 73). In the *first machine age*, when photographs were analogue and created using halide and other chemicals, photograph giants Kodak at one point directly employed some 145,300 people to process and create photographs. However, while digitalization has increased the convenience and quantity of photography, it has also 'profoundly changed the economics of photography production and distribution' (Brynjolfsson and McAfee, 2016: 73). These photos are all now digital, so the hundreds of thousands of people who once worked making photography chemicals and paper must find some other way to support themselves. In contrast, today a team of just fifteen people at Instagram created a 'simple app that over 130 million customers use to share some sixteen billion photos (and counting)' (Brynjolfsson and McAfee, 2016: 73). On the other hand, Kodak recently filed for bankruptcy. The difference is staggering. Brynjolfsson and McAfee (2016) explain that photography is not an isolated example in this shift. Similar shifts have taken place in music and media, finance, publishing, distribution, manufacturing and retail (Brynjolfsson and McAfee, 2016).

Summary

This chapter examined universal basic income in relation to the changing patterns of work. Drawing on Standing (2015a) and others, it described the notion of 'precarious work' and the implications this had on social justice and social equality – particularly for increasing numbers of precarious workers who are subject to insecure, unprotected and poorly paid working conditions. It looked at how a universal basic income could rescue the problems with 'poverty traps' and 'precarity traps' outlined by Standing (2017). It challenged the Thatcherite and Victorian ideas of the 'work ethic' as these traditional ways of thinking about work are inept for the precarious and neoliberal economy we have today. Instead, this chapter outlined Gorz's (1999) argument, which focussed on 'real work' as the whole creative scope of human activity (not merely limited to the things do when 'at work'). This chapter also looked at technological unemployment and the problems of deskilling (Braverman, 1998) and the rise of automation (see Stern, 2016). Drawing on Brynjolfsson and McAfee (2016) this chapter examined how the digital age is rapidly changing the economy in which we live, showing how new technologies can unintentionally lead to adverse consequences for employment. Following Stern (2016) and others, these technological factors offer more reason why a universal basic income can bring stability and security to people's lives.

References

Beynon, H. (1973) *Working for Ford*. London: Penguin.

Booth, R. (2016) 'Uber appeals against ruling that its UK drivers are workers'. *The Guardian*, 14 December. Retrieved from www.theguardian.com/tech nology/2016/dec/14/uber-appeals-against-ruling-that-its-uk-drivers-a re-employees

Braverman, H. (1998) *Labour and Monopoly Capitalism: The Degradation of Work in the Twentieth Century*. New York: Monthly Review Press (first published in 1974).

Brynjolfsson, E. and McAfee, A. (2016) *The Second Machine Age: Work Progress, and Prosperity in a Time of Brilliant Technologies*. New York: Norton and Company.

Etzioni, A. (1986) 'The fast-food factories: McJobs are bad for kids'. *The Washington Post*, 24 August.

Gorz, A. (1999) *Reclaiming Work*. Cambridge: Polity Press.

Gould, A. M. (2010) 'Working at McDonalds: Some redeeming features of "McJobs"'. *Work, Employment and Society*, 24(4): 780–802.

Levitas, R. (2005) *The Inclusive Society? Social Exclusion and New Labour*. Basingstoke: Palgrave Macmillan.

McDonough, B. (2017) 'Precarious work in Europe'. In: S. Isaacs, ed. *European Social Problems*. London: Routledge.

McDonough, B., Foley, A., Ginsburg, N., Isaacs, S., Silverstone, D. and Young, T. (2015) *Social Problems in the UK: An Introduction*. London: Routledge.

Rifkin, J. (1995) *The End of Work: The Decline of the Global Labour Force and the Dawn of the Post-Market Era*. New York: Penguin.

Rotenberg, L., Harter-Griep, R., Fischer, F. M., Fonseca, M. de J. and Landsbergis, P. (2008) *Working at Night and Work Ability among Nursing Personnel: When Precarious Employment Makes the Difference*. New York: Springer.

Standing, G. (2015a) *The Precariat: A New Dangerous Class*. London: Bloomsbury.

Standing, G. (2015b) 'Why basic income's emancipatory value exceeds its monetary value'. *Basic Income Studies*, 10(2): 193–223.

Standing, G. (2017) *Basic Income: And How We Can Make It Happen*. London: Penguin.

Stern, A. (2016) *Raising the Floor: How a Universal Basic Income can Renew our Economy and Rebuild the American Dream*. New York: Perseus Books.

Taylor, F. (2011) *The Principles of Scientific Management*. New York: Prism Key Press.

Torry, M. (2016) *Citizen's Basic Income: A Christian Social Policy*. London: Policy Press.

4

EXAMPLES AND EXPERIMENTS

Introduction

Where can we find examples of universal basic income? And what can real examples tell us about the nature of a universal basic income? This chapter examines classic and contemporary examples of universal basic income found in countries all over the world. Some of these examples are taken from wealthy nations (such as Canada and the US) while other examples are taken from poorer countries (such as India, Namibia and Kenya). This chapter shows that a universal basic income can have varied effects on recipients, depending on the economic, social and political circumstances of the community in which it is implemented. The examples provided in this chapter have been selected to illuminate key aspects of basic income which are discussed in public debate: affordability; productivity; tackling poverty and social equality; health and wellbeing, and other aspects which have been discussed elsewhere in this book. This chapter includes a discussion of one of the world's largest basic income experiments, based in Madhya Pradesh, India, in which more than 6,000 people from twenty villages benefitted from a basic cash income. Some other current examples include the case of Finland, one of the first countries in Europe to launch a universal basic income pilot, in which over a two-year period, two thousand unemployed citizens between the ages of 25 and 58, received 560 euros a month. Current pilots also include those in Ontario, Canada and the GiveDirectly experiments in Kenya and Uganda, as well as Namibia's BIG (Basic Income Grant) project. The chapter also looks at historical examples of basic income pilots or experiments, such as the 1970s Manitoba (US) study and the case of Alaska, an oil-rich state (also in the US), in which a Permanent Fund Dividend (PFD) is paid to Alaska residents living within the state – not technically a basic income but it is a minimum salary distributed to every citizen, regardless of age, employment, or social standing.

Using pilots and experiments for universal basic income

In this text, as in discussions elsewhere of basic income, the terms 'pilot' and 'experiment' are readily used to describe the overall approach or method used to test a basic income. Some use these terms interchangeably. However, it is important to distinguish some differences between pilots and experiments on universal basic income. A full basic income *pilot* usually adopts the full principles of universal basic income, but might be temporally limited or applied to a subset of the wider population – a town, city or region for example – while an *experiment* would usually test certain aspects of a universal basic income, such as its impact on work and unemployment, health and illness, or education and learning. Experiments are not full pilots because they are not 'universal' – they only usually target a particular group. Experiments also usually have elements of conditionality and do not usually meet all the criteria of what is generally deemed as a universal basic income. And so, although media reports often describe certain countries as having piloted a basic income few cases manifest every characteristic of a basic income. The Basic Income Earth Network (BIEN) defines basic income as 'a periodic cash payment unconditionally delivered to all on an individual basis, without means test or work requirement' (see https://basicincome.org). Supporters of a universal basic income argue that it cannot be properly evaluated in a pilot or experiment since a basic income is lifelong while experiments are bounded in duration (Standing, 2017) and thus any social policy experiment would fail to genuinely test a basic income. Universal basic income experiments are contradictory in the sense that they usually focus on a group or sample of people, while a genuine basic income is given to all citizens, so they're not at all 'universal'. While describing and evaluating some of the basic income experiments in this chapter it is wise to be aware of the limitations and dynamics which experiments usually entail. The implementation of basic income, during an experiment, usually requires an evaluation of the impact the basic income has had on recipients, their families and their communities. But the impact of such an experiment is difficult to measure and understand. Some evaluations might show the immediate effects a basic income has on the individual recipient. But not all changes in behaviour and attitudes of a community are immediate and many effects of introducing a basic income may take a long time to see (Devala et al., 2015). However, while we must be cautious in understanding the pilots and experiments of a universal basic income, we can also learn a lot about what a basic income can do from examining them in this chapter.

What follows is a series of examples – some of which are basic income pilot studies or experiments, and some which are neither yet have resonance with basic income. To date, there has not been one *fully implemented* case of universal basic income anywhere in the world. Indeed, most cases presented in this chapter are not considered as universal basic income in the strictest sense, but instead have resonance with its principles and share many of its characteristics. All of the examples that follow have been selected as 'food for thought', and are told as a set of narratives which contextualize as much as possible, the circumstances in which universal basic income has been tried and tested. The array of examples allow readers to look at different aspects of a universal basic income and to understand how one might work in practice in different sorts of societies. Given the scope and limitations of this text, it has not been possible to examine every case of universal basic income, from all over the world and in every detail. However, the selected examples in this chapter are extremely useful for readers of basic income, many of which have already been discussed among scholars, policy-makers and politicians.

Is it affordable? Paying for a universal basic income

Affordability is one of the most important factors when discussing the potential success of a universal basic income (Standing, 2017). Most governments want to understand what the 'right amount' of income is for families to live above the poverty line, while also quantifying how much these amounts will cost the state (or the taxpayer). In 2016 in Britain, economists Stewart Lansley and Howard Reed published a report on Universal Basic Income for left-wing think-tank Compass. They said that the cost of a Universal Basic Income for the British population (some 66 million people) could be as high as £300 billion, but that most of this could be made afforded by using existing welfare spending covered by existing taxes, or with only minor tax raises. An additional £28 billion may be required, but this merely means returning to British welfare spending levels of 2010. However, others have questioned the affordability of a universal basic income. For example, Caroline Lucas, from UK's Green party, said that a 'citizen's wage' – has long been party policy, but it did not make the cut for their manifesto because they couldn't find a way to fund it. Concerns over the affordability of a basic income are commonplace. To provide every citizen with regular cash sums requires large amounts of revenue to be generated from somewhere – usually from the taxation of those working. But one purpose of a universal basic income is also to free people from ungratifying employment – providing more flexibility and choice to work. Thus there is a problem with funding a universal basic income if those providing the resources through taxation fail to work. Most supporters of basic income welcome the flexibility to work, 'unless it dries up the source on which the funding of basic income depends' (Van Parijs and Vanderborght, 2017: 133). Some critics of a basic income believe that it would lead to lower wages, because employers would not need to pay as much, knowing that workers have another source of income. However, advocates of basic income argue that it would 'give people greater ability to refuse exploitative wage offers and more confidence to bargain for higher wages' (Standing, 2017: 121). The wages of people is central to the sustainability of a universal basic income if it is the taxation of labour which ultimately pays for the scheme to work. But there are examples of revenue generation which is not dependent on the taxation of wages. One example of this is Alaska's Permanent Fund Dividend (USA). Alaska, an oil rich state, uses its oil revenue to give residents a payout every year, based on oil revenues over five year periods. For example, in 2015, every resident who met the conditions for the benefit received $2,072 of income for the year. Although Alaska is a relatively expensive state in which to live, this income given, by virtue of being a citizen, is one of the highest in any state or country in the world. In contrast to other states in the US, Alaska appears to be the most egalitarian, providing a share of its wealth with every citizen (Van Parijs and Vanderborght, 2017). There is controversy over whether we can call Alaska's Permanent Fund Dividend a universal basic income, but it is certainly one example of how the wealth of natural resources can be shared out to benefit all citizens in society, showing how a basic income in wealthier nations could be provided in an affordable way. Interestingly, Alaska's scheme was introduced by a Republican administration, who said that the dividend program was anything but socialistic (see Van Parijs and Vanderborght, 2017: 94–95). Alaska's Constitution holds that its natural resources are owned by the people, not by the state, as with forms of socialism. It is the people of Alaska who determine how to spend the money, rather than the state, according to the Alaskan administration.

Another example which has resonance with Alaska's Permanent Fund Dividend is Iran's Nationwide Cash Subsidy Scheme. Although a cash subsidy is not a basic income, Iran's scheme launched in 2010 does share some, if not most of its features: paid by the government; universal; unconditional; regular and pays the same amount to all citizens. The scheme was launched out of discontent with an inefficient fuel subsidies system and did not necessarily emerge from basic income ideals, such as around freedom and alleviating poverty. But despite not intending to be a basic income as such, the Nationwide Cash Subsidy Scheme does come far closer to a universal basic income than most other large-scale cash transfer schemes in the world. Importantly, Iran's Nationwide Cash Subsidy Scheme is affordable because it relies on oil as a natural resource of the country, from which all citizens can benefit. National revenues are partially distributed to the entire country's population (citizens of Iran). This is done in cash, on a regular basis, unconditionally and for an indefinite period of time. All citizens are entitled to the same amount regardless. It is the largest and most generous programme of its kind, initially transferring $500 a year per capita, reaching some 72.5 million people. The intention is to provide 15% of national income through cash transfers to households. Although all individuals are entitled to benefit, payments are made to every head of household on their behalf – which can arguably disadvantage women who become dependent on their husbands to receive the income (see Chapter 5 for a discussion of universal basic income and women). Furthermore, foreigners living in Iran are not eligible for transfers, even if the loss of subsidies will affect them as much as other citizens. Contrary to the expectation that a basic income could only be possible in more developed countries, Iran, as a developing Middle Eastern and Islamic country, has become one of the pioneers of a 'basic income' scheme. However, it is also important to note that due to some of its features, for example its scale and amount of resource needed, the scheme may not be a sustainable program over the long term.

Impact on poverty and social inequalities

A universal basic income can tackle poverty and social inequalities related to needs such as basic food, shelter and housing; health and wellbeing and access to education. In one of the world's largest ever basic income experiments, carried out in rural areas of Madhya Pradesh, India, a number of improvements to the lives of basic income recipients can be examined. In 2009–2010, UNICEF funded and supported by a local organization called the Self Employed Woman's Association (SEWA) the experiment evaluated the impact unconditional transfers, or basic income grants would have on communities consisting of about 6,000 men, women and children (Devala et al., 2015). For eighteen months, recipients would receive a cash sum which could be spent however they wished. This was the first time a basic income (one which was unconditional and universal) was trialled in India. The recipients situation before, during and after receiving the grants was evaluated by three rounds of statistical surveys and case studies, comparing all the changes during the period with a control group that did not receive the grants. There were two pilots. The first was called MPUCT (Madhya Pradesh Unconditional Transfer), which involved eight villages in which everybody received monthly grants. Twelve villages were used as control villages. The second pilot was called TVUCT (Tribal Village Unconditional Cash Transfer). This involved providing grants to everybody in one tribal village, with one other tribal village as a comparison. The trials aimed at identifying the effects of a basic income on individual and family behaviour and attitudes. In the selected villages, every man, woman and child was provided with a modest unconditional grant each month. Initially, in the larger project, every adult received 200 rupees a month and every child 100 rupees. After a year these amounts were raised to 300 and 150 rupees a month respectively. In the tribal village, the amounts were 300 and 150 rupees for the entire year. This meant that an average family earned the equivalent of $24 per month. The amount given was calculated based on working out what was a quarter of the income of median-income families, at just above the current poverty line.

The basic income trials in the villages of Madhya Pradesh tackled poverty and social inequality in a number of ways. In terms of *housing*, families that received the basic income 'were more likely to make small but cumulatively significant changes to their housing and living conditions' (Devala et al., 2015). This included in some cases being able to improve 'the house' (dwelling) itself, by fixing or upgrading roofs for example. But it also included buying household assets, including bicycles and motorbikes, enabling family members to get to and from work more easily. In terms of *education*, the unconditional basic income facilitated and encouraged more intensive schooling and helped to block a number of constraints to education of the young. One woman, who was a wage labourer from the SEWA village of Jagmalpipliya, explained how the basic income helped to send her children to school:

> My husband passed away two months ago due to a kidney failure, and because of that our condition has become very bad. My only source of income is casual labour, which also is not available regularly. Our main expenditure is on food. I buy food items for only five to ten days because I have very little money. My eldest son is 20 years old. He and I are the only two people who go to work in my family. My three other sons go to school. They get lunch in the school, and they recently got money for their uniform. After my husband's demise, my son Nerendra and I increased our hours of labour, but one of my sons is mentally challenged, so he is not able to do much labour. Employers easily exploit him. Three of my boys are studying and we have to bear the expenditure for their education. This money has helped us a lot. If it were not for

it, we would have had to send our children for labour work. But because of this money we are able to send them to school.

(Cited in Devala et al., 2015: 135)

The basic income enabled some families to change the circumstances in which they lived. But this was not the same for everyone in the Madhya Pradesh experiment. Some recipients were resigned to taking their children out of school despite the implementation of the basic income (Devala et al., 2015). The basic income experiments of Madhya Pradesh helped tackle inequalities in regards to *health and nutrition* too. Food deficiency fell, diets were more nutritious, and there was a shift from the reliance of ration shops to the market and own production of food. Child nutrition in particular improved, tested by the weight-for-age measures (Devala et al., 2015). Improvements in nutrition affected capabilities, enabling children to attend school more regularly, boosting economic growth, and enabling adults to be more productive in the world of work. Importantly, these social factors, when improved, worked accumulatively to enhance the wellbeing of individuals, families and whole communities, which has a knock-on effect for the future offspring of these families too.

Overall, the basic income experiments in Madhya Pradesh yielded a number of positive results, including better nutrition, lower debt, greater job opportunities, higher rates of school attendance for children, and better healthcare. The impact on women was particularly empowering, as having an income given directly to women provided more independence, thus providing more gender equality.

Impact on work, productivity and economic activities

If we examine the affect universal basic income has on work, economic growth and productivity, we find there are several examples that illustrate how basic income can stimulate economic activity. Contrary to the idea that 'free cash' will dissuade people from entering full-time employment and therefore stifle economic growth, many basic income examples provide evidence to show that communities can become more prosperous from the implementation of a universal basic income, with recipients of a basic income more likely to want to engage in paid work or profit-making activities. For example, in Ethiopia, a USAID two-year basic income scheme was developed in response to a severe drought which created severe poverty. Evaluations of the scheme showed that the modest income grants helped people to cut their debts, make modest investments in improving their capabilities and productivity and rebuild their livelihoods. The investment made by USAID led to significant improvement to the lives of those receiving the basic income. Some Ethiopian families used the income to invest in sending their children to school. It led to a significant improvement in the capacity for recipients and their family members to work, or develop capabilities of doing so. The income meant that health was more likely to improve and children in those families were more likely to attend school. The chances of members falling ill (both young and old) was reduced because basic nutrition had improved.

Ethiopia is not an isolated example of how a basic income can drive productivity. Between 2007 and 2009, the Namibian Tax Consortium (NAMTAX) implemented a BIG in the Otjivero-Omitara area of Namibia, providing all residents below the age of 60 years a grant of NAD100 per person per month. Namibia's BIG, according to the organizers, led to a moderate increase in economic activity, with the rate of those engaged in income-generating activities (above the age of 15) reportedly increasing from 44% to 55% (see www.bignam.org). The scheme helped some recipients to kick-start their own businesses in food outlets (such as baking bread), construction work (such as brick-laying), and fashion design (such as dress-making). The local economy gained from families having more buying power, boosting the commerce of local markets and in turn alleviating some of the poverty experienced in local communities. Some reports also showed a reduction in child malnutrition, a dramatic improvement in school attendance and a significant reduction in crime.

The BIG pilot project abided by several key principles: it was universal; cash based entitlement; provided income security, and built on the idea of redistributive justice (see also Haarmann and Haarmann, 2012, for a discussion of the BIG pilot project). The project was set up using the direct support of Otjivero-Omitara residents and the community established an 18-member committee to help mobilize people and advise residents on how to spend the BIG money wisely. By the end of the project, there appeared to be several positive outcomes, with the grant impacting upon the Namibian communities in a number of ways, including: better health and nutrition; better clothing; improved transportation, and a rise in entrepreneurship. The grant had a particularly positive effect on poverty. For example, prior to the BIG, 76% of citizens were reported to be below the food poverty line, but this statistic was reduced to 37% within one year of the BIG, and to just 10% by the end of the scheme (www.centreforpublicimpact.org). The BIG was considered to be successful by the Namibian government and a plan was proposed to nationalize the scheme between 2016 and 2025. However, the proposal has yet to be deployed and there now appears to be some reluctance in carrying out a nationwide version of the scheme. Instead, Namibia reverted to traditional methods of trying to alleviate poverty, such as food banks and conditional grants for selected groups. The reasons why the Namibian government sidelined a nationwide universal basic income are unclear, but some critics have alleged that government officials have delayed its development to protect corporate interests, which profit from the cheap labour that poor Namibian communities can provide. Unfortunately, the usual prejudices about basic income have also surfaced in Namibia, such as concerns that the grant would make people lazy and dependent on hand-outs.

In 2008, a Youth Opportunities Program was set up in northern Uganda, to give small groups of young people resources to develop new skills for employment and entrepreneurship. Each recipient received $382 dollars, but it was given with a twist, as the money had to be spent on gaining a skilled trade. Immediate results appeared encouraging, with many of the young people building small businesses, enabling them to transform their lives for themselves and their families. Although not a basic income, this cash injection program provides evidence of how cash incentives can be used to stimulate economic activities, by providing a means with which people can generate income for themselves. In 2017, another project set in Uganda, provided community residents with cash payments in the Ugandan village of Busibi. A Belgian organization called Eights set up an unconditional transfer project providing all residents of the village (including 56 adults and 88 children) monthly cash payments. Each adult receives US$18.25

(about €16.70) per month, approximately 30% of the average income of lower-income families in Uganda, and each child receives half of this amount. The 'unconditional transfer project' (as they have called it) has resonance with a universal basic income, showing why cash is better to alleviate poverty than food handouts. The project also shows how unconditional cash can impact upon women's lives in particular, allowing them access to education, healthcare and a way of achieving economic development through entrepreneurship, without the necessity to marry a man (see also Chapter 5).

In 2016, a basic income experiment was developed in Kenya by the US-based charity GiveDirectly, which provides unconditional cash transfers to the residents of two-hundred villages in rural Kenya (about 26,000 people in total). A pilot study began in which all 95 residents of one village receive monthly unconditional cash payments of about US $23 (€21) per month, amounting to roughly half of the average income in rural Kenya. This unconditional cash payment project is still ongoing at the time of writing this text and results of the program are still being produced, but early results report a number of positive outcomes, with the cash injections boosting the local economy. For example, one recipient of the income moved from the village to the town of Kisumu to open up a haircutting shop. The unconditional cash payments gave her enough income to move into a larger space where she could rent out a room, bringing in even more income, some of which she sent back to her mother in the village to help care for the other children in her extended family. Like examples elsewhere, this case shows that a cash injection helps to bolster economic activities which have knock-on effects for family members and others in the community.

Impacting on health and wellbeing

One of the most important features of a universal basic income is that it can provide basic security. Standing (2017: 91) argues that 'basic security is a human need' and a lack of basic security affects mental and physical health and can reduce the chances of psychological disorders. When people lack basic essentials, such as water, food or money, their preoccupation with trying to find solutions can use up much of their mental energy and can lead to a number of problems, including low self-esteem, anxiety and even depression. A study of long-term cash injections into the local community by a casino company in the US found that the mental health of young people improved as a result of better financial security (Velasquez-Manoff, 2014). When Cherokee Casino Hotel was built in 1997, it agreed to share some of its profits with some of the poorest people in the local community (Smoky Mountains area of North Carolina, US). Several years after the casino hotel had been built researchers from Duke University Medical School found that the profit sharing had positive and long-lasting effects on the mental health of recipients receiving the funds. Young people from some of the poorest families benefitted the most from the profit sharing scheme, with children's rates of depression, anxiety and behavioural problems declining after the families began receiving the cash supplements. Examples like this, illustrate how basic finance can provide basic security, which in turn increases resilience to a range of physical and mental health problems and maintains the general wellbeing of families and communities.

In June 2017, the government of the Canadian province of Ontario initiated a three-year pilot study of a guaranteed minimum income. Official results from the study are expected to be reported in 2020, however, intermediary reports suggest that the pilot study is having a positive effect, particularly for recipients reporting *less stress, better health* and more independence from receiving the income (Standing, 2019). Some four thousand participants were randomly selected from a pool of low-income adults between the ages of 18 and 64 years who have lived in one of the three test locations (Hamilton, Brantford and Brant County regions) for at least one year. Participants in the study received a minimum annual income of $16,989 per year for a single person, less 50% of any earned income. Couples received $24,027 less 50% of any earned income. Those with a disability received an additional $500 per month as well. One woman, who lost her right leg to a chronic bone disease, used the additional income to buy herself a new walker. Allowing her more mobility, the new walker, equipped with 'all the bells and whistles' allowed her to get to the grocery store more regularly (Monsebraaten, 2018: 1). The 'basic income' reportedly gave recipients more independence, with more autonomy to make life style choices to improve their own health and wellbeing. The pilot in

Ontario is commonly called a 'basic income' in Canada. However, although participants in the study can work or study while receiving the income, their basic income amount decreases by $0.50 for every dollar an individual earns, so the program is not a basic income in BIEN's sense, or that proposed in this chapter. Nevertheless, it does have resonance with a universal basic income, showing how the health and wellbeing of people can improve with the introduction of 'cash-for-nothing'. As well as health and health care usage, the government of Ontario are evaluating a number of key areas including employment and labour market participation, education and training, food security and housing stability.

The idea that a basic income can improve health and wellbeing has been a key feature of Finland's *perustulokeilu* (so-called 'basic income' experiment). In January 2017, the national government of Finland launched a 'basic income' experiment designed and implemented by Kela, Finland's Social Insurance Institution. The experiment gave a cash sum of 560 euros per month, over a two year period, to a sample of two thousand people. The recipients were between the ages of 25 and 58 and had been receiving unemployment benefits in November 2016 (from a group of 175,000 potential recipients). Results from the study showed that recipients reported being a lot *happier and less stressed*, although there was little evidence to suggest that a basic income had helped provide the time to secure better (or more desired) forms of employment. Rather than feeling desperate and stressed about a lack of money, recipients felt more secure, knowing that they had a basic level of income to fall back on. Many media reports have been critical of Finland's basic income experiment (one of the largest basic income experiments in Europe). For example, the BBC reported that 'Finland basic income trial left people "happier but jobless"' (Nagesh, 2019), indicating that it failed to positively impact upon recipient's employment prospects despite improving their state of wellbeing. We must bear in mind, however, that the Finnish experiment was pioneered by Finland's center-right, austerity-focused government, which launched a basic income to mainly incentivize people to take up paid employment. Focusing on one key issue (work and unemployment), the Finnish government is arguably more concerned with bringing down the country's unemployment rate (over 8%) than with the values of universal basic income itself – social justice, social equality and freedom (discussions of these concepts are taken up in Chapter 2 of this book). This was why the experiment was aimed at only unemployed people – the Finnish government have not yet experimented beyond this limited group. Existing welfare benefits in Finland, like those in many European countries, suffer from the employment trap – unemployed Finnish citizens are put off taking up employment in fear that the higher marginal tax rates will leave them worse off. The Finnish experiment was designed to find solutions to tackle unemployment and to bolster economic growth. Based on some of its own measures (around increasing employment figures), it has not proved successful, but there are still arguably many other aspects of this experiment which can be said to support a basic income – being happier and mentally healthier is just one of them.

Improvements in the health of a community is also one of the key research finding of the Manitoba Basic Annual Income Experiment (Mincome), conducted in the US during the 1970s. The experiment emerged through concerns about poverty and income inequality and was intended to provide evidence of the feasibility, impact and effectiveness of programs based on some sort of guaranteed basic income. Unfortunately, in 1978, after the federal government became increasingly concerned about the costs of the project, they decided to withdraw from the experiment and much of the data became lost. Some years later, after recovering a number of boxes full of data, some of the key research findings showed, among other things, that 'the payment of the guaranteed income had led to improved health and fewer hospital visits and a considerable "reduction in physician claims for mental health disorders" that suggested the policy would "improve health and social outcomes at the community level"' (Standing, 2019: 60, quoting Forget, 2011). Importantly, the data also showed that recipients felt a greater sense of economic security, and that it 'de-stigmatized income assistance' (Standing, 2019: 60, citing Calinitsky and Latner, 2017).

Giving no strings attached cash to some of the poorest in society has concerned many people. The worry is that poor people will spend a basic income on things which are bad for their health and wellbeing. For example, in attempting to understand the impact Alaska's Permanent Fund Dividend has made to Alaskan residents, a market research company called Harstad Strategic Research conducted a survey, asking how the fund is being spent. While 85% of respondents agreed that 'many people spend a large part of the Permanent Fund dividends on basic needs' and 79% agreed that 'The permanent fund dividend cheques are an important source of income for people in my community', 43% agreed with the statement that: 'Many people have wasted a large part of their Permanent Fund on such things as liquor and drugs'. The issue of how the income is spent is quite important for studies of universal basic income. Some people have criticized giving the fund to some of the poorer or less advantaged Alaskan residents, in fear that it might be wasted on 'alcohol, cigarettes and other "bads" rather than on their children and essentials such as food, clothes and heating' (Standing, 2017: 118–119). But these fears are usually fuelled by stereotypical ideas about 'the working class' and 'the poor' – groups who are considered by some to be unable to make sensible decisions by themselves (Standing, 2017). Overall, and as the examples above have shown, people who are given a basic income usually invest in their health and wellbeing, if given the opportunity to.

Summary

This chapter discussed a range of issues, such as affordability; productivity; poverty; social equality; health, and wellbeing, by examining a broad range of 'basic income' examples. Some of these examples were full basic income pilots, while, adopting the full principles of universal basic income, were temporally limited or applied to a subset of the wider population (a town, city or region). Other examples discussed here were experiments, which tested certain aspects of a universal basic income, such as its impact on unemployment, incentive to start a business, or investment in education and learning. Other examples could not be defined as 'universal basic income' at all, but had resonance with some of the ideas basic income entails, such as regular payments of cash, unconditional, given with no strings attached. Alaska's Permanent Fund Dividend (USA) was one such example. It is not a basic income, as it is purely dependent upon the success of oil profit revenue generated and therefore the amount alters every year, with the amount usually not enough to take families above the poverty line. But like Iran's Nationwide Cash Subsidy Scheme, it showed us how revenue from natural resources could be redistributed to provide an income to people society-wide. Because such funds are given to everyone, it is a scheme usually welcomed by all in society.

This chapter examined how a universal basic income can help combat poverty and social inequalities. We drew examples from the basic income experiments of Madhya Pradesh, India, some of the largest basic income experiments to have ever taken place. We saw that basic income could help people in terms of housing; education, and health and nutrition. The experiments in India showed that people are more than capable of making spending decisions which would improve the social and economic situations of themselves, their children and their families. Standing (2017) argues that many other cash transfer schemes around the world involve elaborate conditions imposed on recipients. Despite such conditions being well meant, he argues that such conditions are often not applied fairly and involve high administrative costs (Standing, 2017). Imposing conditions generally require beneficiaries to 'prove' they had fulfilled those conditions through a legal process. A genuine universal basic income has no such red tape, and is available for everyone without complex legal processes or bureaucracy, as proved successful in the experiments of Madhya Pradesh.

This chapter also saw how basic income can help get people into work, enhance productivity and provide economic growth to entire communities. Examples taken from Ethiopia's USAID two-year basic income scheme showed that modest income grants helped people to cut their debts and invest in their futures to improve their own skills and capabilities. With Namibia's BIG project, people used the income to kick-start their own businesses in a range of industries, from dressmaking to baking. Likewise, the Eights unconditional transfer project in Uganda achieved economic development through entrepreneurship, enabling some marginalized groups (such as women) the capabilities to support themselves independently. Kenya's GiveDirectly unconditional cash transfer scheme provided yet another example of how an income could be used to boost the local economy, with some families able to relocate to bigger towns to set up business.

The chapter showed that a basic income could provide a means of supporting basic security, with basic health and wellbeing at the centre of stability in people's lives. We examined Ontario's guaranteed minimum income study, which had given many Canadian people an opportunity to invest in their health and wellbeing, giving them more independence and providing a stronger foundation with which they could go on to develop their lives. But we also looked at Finland's *perustulokeilu*, which although did not show to have profound effects on work and employment, it did show that a basic income can reduce stress and made people happier and more positive. The benefits of a universal basic income move beyond the need to enable people more choice to pick 'the right' occupation, or to bolster unemployment rates. On the contrary, the necessity to provide a means of living a healthy and stress-free existence is as just important, if not more important, to the principles rooted in a universal basic income.

The examples of universal basic income provided in this chapter are just a handful of the many experiments, trials and case studies of basic income happening all over the world. As readers of these studies, we must always be mindful of the political context in which these examples emerge, understanding the motivations behind the experiments and/or policies which are put in place. This chapter should serve as a 'food for thought' resource which students and others studying universal basic income can use to make sense of basic income, showing both of its potential and drawbacks.

References

Berman, M. (2018) 'Resource rents, universal basic income and poverty amongst Alaska's indigenous peoples'. *World Development*, 16, pp. 161–172.

Bernstein, J. (2014) 'The transfer of income to poor families with children can be an investment with long term payoffs'. *On the Economy*, 19 January.

Bruenig, M. (2014) 'A Cherokee tribe's basic income success story'. *Policy Shop*, 19 January.

Calinitsky, D. and Latner, J. P. (2017) 'Basic income in a small town: Understanding the elusive effects on work'. *Social Problems*, 64(3), pp. 373–397.

Devala, S., Jhabvala, R., Mehta, S. K. and Standing, G. (2015) *Basic Income: A Transformative Policy for India*. Bloomsbury: London.

Forget, E. (2011) 'The town with no poverty: The health effects of a Canadian Guaranteed Annual Income field experiment'. *Canadian Public Policy*, 37(3), pp. 283–305.

Haarmann, C. and Haarmann, D. (2012) 'Namibia: Seeing the sun rise – the realities and hopes of the Basic Income Grant pilot project'. In: M. Murray and C. Pateman, eds. *Basic Income Worldwide*. Basingstoke: Palgrave Macmillan. Monsebraaten, L. (2018) 'From "barely surviving" to thriving: Ontario basic income recipients report less stress, better health'. *The Star*, 24 February. Retrieved from www.thestar.com/news/gta/2018/02/24/from-barely-surviving-to-thriving-ontario-basic-income-recipients-report-less-stress-better-health.html

Munnell, A. (1987) 'Lessons from the income maintenance experiments: an overview'. *New England Economic Review*, May, pp. 32–45. Retrieved from https://aspe.hhs.gov/report/overview-final-report-seattle-denver-income-maintenance-experiment

Nagesh, A. (2019) 'Finland basic income trial left people "happier but jobless"'. Retrieved from www.bbc.co.uk/news/world-europe-47169549

Reed, H. and Lansley, S. (2016) *Universal Basic Income: An Idea whose Time Has Come?* London: Compass. Retrieved from www.compassonline.org.uk/wp-content/uploads/2016/05/UniversalBasicIncomeByCompass-Spreads.pdf

Salehi-Isfahani, D. and Mostafavi-Dehzooei, M. (2018) 'Cash transfers and labor supply: Evidence from a large-scale program in Iran'. *Journal of Development Economics*, 135, pp. 349–367.

Simpson, W.Mason, G. and Godwin, R. (2017) 'The Manitoba Basic Annual Income experiment: Lessons learned 40 years later'. *Canadian Public Policy*, 43 (1), pp. 85–104. Retrieved from https://basicincome.org/news/2017/12/basic-income-guarantee-experiments-1970s-quick-summary-results

Standing, G. (2013) 'Unconditional Basic Income: Two pilots in Madhya Pradesh'. Background note prepared for conference, Delhi, 30–31 May.

Standing, G. (2017) *Basic Income: And How We Can Make It Happen*. London: Penguin.

Standing, G. (2019) *Basic Income as Common Dividends: Piloting a Transformative Policy*. London: Progressive Economy Forum.

Tabatabai, H. (2011) 'The basic income road to reforming Iran's price subsidies'. *Basic Income Studies*, 6(1).

Van Parijs, P. and Vanderborght, Y. (2017) *Basic Income: A Radical Proposal for a free Society and a Sane Economy*. Cambridge, MA: Harvard University Press.

Velasquez-Manoff, M. (2014) 'What happens when the poor receive a stipend?' *New York Times*, 18 January.

5

THE WORK OF WOMEN AND UNIVERSAL BASIC INCOME

Introduction

This chapter discusses the arguments concerning the work of women with an emphasis on feminist perspectives to the issue of a universal basic income. It explores how a universal basic income might have different effects on women's lives and gender inequalities, with a potential for changing the economic and social experiences of women in various social contexts. In some of these cases discussed, the chapter explores how a universal basic income can provide women with financial independence, allowing them a new means of 'freedom'. But this chapter shall also explore how the implementation of a universal basic income can have varying effects on women from diverse backgrounds and identities. It will discuss the potential a universal basic income has in promoting equal rights for men and women and how this would challenge the institutionalized and disadvantaged relationship between work and welfare as experienced by women of different ethnicities, age, cultures and social class positions.

Drawing on feminist economic and social science perspectives, this chapter shall first examine how a universal basic income might increase women's autonomy, economic power and independence. The chapter will then explore how a universal basic income might impact on the roles of women as carers. This looks at the controversy of a universal basic income for women in the home, examining the notion of gender inequality and how a gender-symmetry lifestyle may be undermined by a policy intended for good. The chapter then introduces and develops the notion of intersectionality as a useful way to understand women's situations and lives and how intersectionality can expand the debates around how a universal basic income can impact on the lives of women, focusing on some examples of women living in various parts of the globe.

Gender and citizenship: 'equality versus difference' debate

A universal basic income is connected to the notion of citizenship. Every citizen is entitled to a universal basic income regardless of gender. However, historically speaking, the rights of citizenship have been a privilege largely for men, with women on the peripheral to achieving the same rights and participation as their male counterparts. Some feminists have exposed the quintessential maleness of citizenship (Lister, 2003; Dobrowolsky, 2010), highlighting the ways in which women have been excluded in terms of political participation and rights – consider legal rights to vote and to own property for instance. The rights of women within the notion of citizenship are made complex by the 'dilemmas faced by women in their efforts to juggle unpaid or underpaid work in the home and work outside it, exposing the differential validation of the acutely gendered caring versus earning realms' (Dobrowolsky, 2010: 297). Ruth Lister (2003) examines how there might be a re-gendering of citizenship to improve women's position. However, there are different approaches to re-gendering citizenship (Lister, 2003). First, there is a gender-neutrality approach, most commonly associated with liberal feminism. Here, the emphasis is on equal rights and equal obligations, whereby the gender of the citizen should become irrelevant to the rights and obligations of each member. From this perspective, the priority is to enable women to compete on equal terms with men in the labour market, for example by providing social insurance schemes and having effective sex discrimination and equal pay legislation. A gender-neutrality approach also prioritizes 'family-friendly' employment laws and practices which enable women to combine paid work with caring responsibilities (Lister, 2003). One vision of this is the 'genderless' (Moller-Okin, 1991) family and society in which men and women take equal roles and responsibilities in the home (private sphere) as well as at work. From this perspective, there is a more equitable domestic division of labour allowing men and women to participate in society as equals. Second, there is an approach called 'gender differentiation', which emphasizes women's differences from men. Rather than pushing for sameness, this approach highlights the need for understanding difference between the genders. For example, in relation to childcare responsibilities, women can be proud mothers, provided with time and space to partake in mothering responsibilities. Some feminist writers are critical of this approach. For example, Pateman (2004) argues that this approach creates sexually segregated norms of citizenship which have served to subordinate and marginalize women as political citizens. Pateman (2004: 89) also highlights in her work how a universal basic income can offer a democratic right not to be employed and can help challenge the patriarchal reinforcement of the institution of marriage, employment as the best practice of citizenship. In general, this represents an ongoing 'equality versus difference' debate within feminist thinking. Lister (2003) identifies a third position, a gender-pluralist citizen. Here the focus is on understanding the multiple forms in which women are oppressed within subordinated positions. This has resonance with the idea of intersectionality – how gender also intersects with categories like social class, age and ethnicity, which we shall revisit in the discussion of intersectionality throughout this chapter.

Increasing women's autonomy, economic power and independence

There are many arguments for implementing a universal basic income, and although the idea still remains controversial, it has gathered momentum, particularly among feminists. At present, there is no single feminist approach to universal basic income, but there are many arguments which discuss the introduction of a universal basic income and the impact this would have on the lives of women. This is because of the potential in which a universal basic income 'offers women a financial base that does not depend on their partaking in the wages of men' (O'Brien, 2017: 99). As a result, it allows them greater autonomy, providing them with more scope to live independently, at whatever stage of their lives. On this basis a universal basic income can provide a form of economic independence which empowers women (O'Brien, 2017), potentially improving women's 'civil, social, cultural, economic, financial and political rights' (Devala et al., 2015: 159). The proposal of a universal basic income which is defined as an unconditional cash benefit that is paid to every individual and not to households is open to debate. Standing (2017) deals with some of the initial controversies around a universal basic income which have arisen as the proposals gain international interest. On 'universal', Standing (2017: 4) discusses some of the concerns around who is truly eligible and how this is an issue to be decided through democratic processes, which would present some interesting questions as to who is regarded as a citizen. On 'basic' we need to consider how high a universal basic income should be, and whether it should be enough for just mere survival, or also for participation in society more fully (Standing, 2017: 3–4). Most importantly, within the proposals around basic income if a universal basic income is paid to individuals; this would include women, regardless of their marital or employment status, or whether their households or spouses are in receipt of welfare benefits. This is an important and different approach to current benefit payments such as universal credit in the UK, which for couples combines all benefit entitlements, and is paid through one single monthly payment, into one single account. However, this approach has been criticized because of its potential for abuse; if a universal basic income is paid directly to women (and men), as individuals, this could make it easier for those domestically abused to get out of violent or abusive relationships (O'Brien, 2017). The idea of a universal basic income has also been gathering some political momentum. To this effect, political parties such as the Green party in the UK disagree with the single payments to households – as it happens through universal credit- rather than to individuals, and have expressed their support for a universal basic income.

Feminists scholars (McKay, 2005; McLean, 2016; Zelleke, 2011) who are in support of an income maintenance fund, such as universal basic income, have proposed how this regular payment will contribute to women's autonomy, increase their economic power and independence, as well as re-balance many of the gender inequalities that continue to exist in society. Other feminist scholars (Robeyns, 2010; Gheaus, 2008) are less enthusiastic about the idea of a universal basic income and suggest that it will not help diminish the gendered division of labour, or reduce the gender pay gap, nor increase the participation of women in employment markets. For example, Gheaus (2008: 3) argues that 'should a BI be introduced, it would be reasonable to expect an overall drop in female labour ... differing income effects for different groups of women ... and a drop in women's bargaining power within the household, decreased self-esteem and loss of social capital'. In other words, Gheaus suggests that women may be more likely to give up full-time careers in the world of work, knowing that there's a sustainable means in which they can base themselves at home, overseeing caring and domestic responsibilities.

Feminist views on universal basic income although varied, recognize that a universal basic income will have important effects on poverty, but might not contribute substantially to shift structural inequalities around gender. While many women may benefit from such a policy reform, it is not clear whether or not a universal basic income has the potential to really 'transform the patriarchal capitalist state' (O'Brien, 2017: 100). Drawing on feminist arguments for and against a universal basic income, this chapter examines the lives of women from an inter-sectional perspective to understand the multilayered social influences and constraints which women with diverse identities experience.

A universal basic income has the potential to alleviate the problems associated with the 'benefit trap', in which benefit recipients can often be worse off financially when seeking employment, or moving from benefits into employment. This situation affects more women than men and has a bigger impact on women than men for two key reasons. First, because women are still seen as the primary carers of children and the elderly, they are, as a social group, more likely than men to find themselves in this predicament. Second, the 'benefit trap' has a more significant impact on women because the lowest paid jobs in society are still largely occupied by women. And so, when women attempt to seek employment (whether this is part-time or full-time), they are more likely to be offered lower-paid and low-status jobs than their male counterparts. Women still dominate sectors of employment which are traditionally low-paid, such as retail or secretarial work, pastoral or care work. Furthermore, women are more likely to occupy part-time work than men, with such jobs characterized by poor pay, insecurity and a lack of fringe benefits (Schulz, 2017). While a universal basic income will not eradicate all inequalities, it does have the potential to increase women's autonomy, by providing some economic power and independence from men. Despite some key drawbacks discussed in this section, a universal basic income can empower woman in many aspects of their day-to-day lives, as we shall see in the following sections of this chapter.

Women as carers: supporting or undermining gender equality?

Another important debate to have surfaced from the arguments discussed above is the extent to which the state continues to ignore the work carried out by women in the privacy of the home, such as, the caring for children, ill relatives and the elderly and other work which does not have any recognized remuneration. Many of the feminist debates around universal basic income have considered the impact it could have on caregivers, a group which is overwhelmingly female (O'Brien, 2017; Schulz, 2017). Caregivers provide an enormous value to society and yet their work is largely unrecognized. This in itself is a result of care work being regarded as women's work – women and the activities carried out by women are regarded as less important than the activities of men. Receiving a universal basic income would minimize the financial loss caregivers have from not taking part in the paid labour market – making their decision to look after the others less of an economic sacrifice. Many arguments around universal basic income also consider its benefits for women who have taken breaks from employment due to homemaking or raising children, bringing a level of equality to activities that have historically been undervalued.

However, other issues become central to feminist scholars when we think of women as caregivers. For example, Orloff (2013) points out that while a universal basic income might improve women's economic position, spending power and overall economic independence, it does very little in challenging the social norms which construct women as exclusively responsible for homemaking and domestic work. Orloff is very sceptical of the potential universal basic income might have in helping women who are caregivers to go out into other forms of paid employment. Potentially, universal basic income could be seen as a very tangible factor in continuing women's attachment to the home and in the role of caregivers; making it more difficult for women to pursue other types of employment, and therefore having little impact on the gendered division of labour. Put simply, providing women with a regular cash income will not encourage them to leave the home, which unfortunately maintains the existing gender roles of men and women. More women may want to stay home, raising their children and living the housewife role which feminists have campaigned against for so many decades (see Oakley, 1974). Another important factor to consider is that women who are full-time carers or homemakers are more likely to live in poverty and so a universal basic income might help in providing a basic sustenance, but not help in lifting them out of poverty; something that is more likely to happen if women pursue other types of paid work (O'Brien, 2017).

Further considering whether a universal basic income will give equality to women, the term 'gender symmetry' has also been used to evaluate the possible impacts it can have on women's lives. Gheaus (2008: 2) points to how a society that is 'gender just' should measure the level of equality that exists in how possible it is to lead gender-symmetrical life: 'a gender-symmetrical lifestyle is one in which women and men engage equally in paid work and family life, which includes unpaid care work for dependants'. The notion of gender symmetry is interesting since it provides a response to the problems that have historically characterized the patterns of care and work that mark women's and men's lives. As a wider aspect of gender justice, women are often treated unequally as they continue to hold some exclusive responsibility over the care of children and the family. Gheaus is proposing that encouraging gender-symmetrical lives is very important in sustaining social justice for men and women, but this requires that we define work differently: 'work includes market and non-market activities that are productive of goods or services, and "family" includes various long-term living arrangements based on emotional attachments, typically involving extended periods of dependency related to child care, old age, illness and sometimes life-long disabilities' (Gheaus, 2008: 3). Therefore, recognizing that 'work' is not just related to employment markets and outwards, more public activities, but also with caring for home matters in the privacy of the home. Thus, a key question is: will a universal basic income encourage gender-symmetrical lives?

While the work of Gheaus (2008) proposes a more balanced approach to the definition of work and the participation of men in aspects of care and homemaking, it does not challenge the current devaluing of women's work, and the unrecognized status of child rearing and childcare as important activities that contribute to society and the economy. Within the notion of gender-symmetrical lifestyles there is still an implicit division between family only and work only domains, as separate and intrinsically gendered, with men retaining the image of the breadwinner and women retaining the image of the homemaker. Also, the focus of this view of gender justice is more aligned to women who experience a more 'normative' family life, with a spouse or partner who is also employed or financially viable. This becomes evident in the claims made on how a universal basic income would encourage women to drop out of career paths and make women's exit from domesticity harder:

> Given current cultural norms, it is likely that women will be expected to shoulder the burden of private care, especially if they will indeed gradually be more excluded from the market. The privatization of care and the confinement of more women to domesticity fare badly for gender justice for a number of reasons. Economically, women will lose skills and social capital, making their re-entry in the market increasingly difficult – ultimately, many will have no substantive exit right from domesticity.
>
> *(Gheaus, 2008: 5)*

However, it is important to problematize this suggested mass decrease in women's participation in labour markets, if a universal basic income were introduced, as many women in well-remunerated and career-centred jobs might not want to give this status up, but instead they might want to improve the work–family balance in their lives, just as their partners might do too. A universal basic income may impact on the roles of men too. In situations where women are the main breadwinners, many men might choose to take charge of domestic and care responsibilities.

The introduction of a universal basic income has potential in bringing a more equal and beneficial impact on women's lives, particularly those women living in poverty, especially single mothers, or women living in within aspects of social vulnerability. Despite this, it is useful to consider gender equality again, with a wider focus on women's lives and how a universal basic income could benefit vulnerable groups in capitalist economies; such as, single mothers and their children. Thinking about whether a universal basic income would enhance or hinder gender equality opens up debates about what we conceive to be gender equality and social justice. As suggested in the previous paragraph the view of gender-symmetrical lives proposes the equal participation of men and women in duties of care and employment. Indeed, gender equality should be about reducing the unequal positions between men and women in duties of care, but it should also be about increasing the participation of women in the distribution of labour. A universal basic income could be a very important step in securing these aspects of gender equality.

In democratic countries with economies based on capitalism the best rewards and opportunities are given to those in employment, particularly those in full-time employment. This position can become difficult for women to fulfil if they need to take time off work to have children or raise their families. But even for women in well-paid jobs it can be more beneficial to stay at home since the costs of childcare bear little correlation with wages and can be too expensive for a family to afford. Also, options for childcare, out of school hours and holidays can be problematic too. Feminist critiques and demands to respond to these issues have argued that these situations hinder gender equality and can be avoided by providing women and families with affordable and flexible models of childcare which allow them to go back to work when they choose to do so (Beem, 2005). However, there is an assumption here that women might make decisions about their working lives always on their own, not taking into account their family situation and their partner's position. Some women, raising children on their own, cannot rely on the financial, social or psychological support of a partner and are therefore at a higher risk of raising their children in poverty, of suffering with mental health issues or experiencing social exclusion (O'Brien, 2017). A universal basic income would benefit both cases and its emphasis on being universal, irrespective of earnings or employment status, would defy the social divisions of class and ethnicity which continue to impact heavily on women's lives.

Another model which has been associated with universal basic income is that of the universal caretaker (Fraser, 1994), which seeks to normalize the caring responsibilities that normally fall upon women's shoulders for everyone in a society. Fraser critiques schemes which seek to reward caregivers with remuneration for their care, making care responsibilities informal work which should be recognized by society with payments. The problem with this approach is not the payment but rather the failure to question the gendered distribution of labour in care roles, with an overwhelming majority undertaken by women. Paying the carer, which is likely to be a woman, will not challenge the gendered divisions that exist between carers and breadwinners. Instead, what Fraser (1994) suggests is to normalize the patterns of life of women in society, without dividing remunerations dependant on whether one is a carer or a worker, or breadwinner; a universal caretaker stipend would assume that caring becomes a shared responsibility and allows all individuals to take part in the crucial activity of caring for others. Similarly, a universal basic income resembles Fraser's proposition by providing individuals with a remuneration which might allow for more shared responsibilities in the home to emerge, but without deepening divisions between paid employment and care work.

While a universal basic income may not rebalance or fully address, all inequalities, it is important to explore the nuances that a universal basic income can have on women's lives. In the next sections the chapter will point to some of the inequalities and exclusions, direct and indirect that women experience because of the prevalence of gender roles and gender patterns that prevail in society and how the notion of intersectionality can be used to illuminate different feminist perspectives on a universal basic income.

Universal basic income and intersectionality

Universal basic income is particularly useful for helping women who experience intersections of inequality. All of the different perspectives from feminist scholars discussed present a particular interpretation of gender equality and what is needed to address gendered divisions of labour. The majority of perspectives construct a category of woman which does not resemble the heterogeneity that is found in women's lives. It is important for students and readers of universal basic income to understand the nuances a universal basic income has country per country, and region per region. The ways in which a universal basic income might have an impact on women can be better illustrated if it is contextualized within intersectionality.

The notion of intersectionality has been used by feminist and anti-racist scholars for a few decades. Introduced in the 1980s it opened up new ways to produce knowledge and understand inequalities in an era marked by various social justice movements. Since then, inter-sectionality has encouraged more interdisciplinarity in various fields including sociology, feminist theory, history, anthropology and politics. Crucially, intersectionality 'exposed how single-axis thinking under-mines legal thinking, disciplinary knowledge production, and struggles for social justice' (Cho et al., 2013: 787). The debates around a uni-versal basic income raising so many considerations around aspects of social justice, social participation, and social inclusion can be enligh-tened by the notion of intersectionality. Intersectionality's potential lies in how it pushes us to examine 'the dynamics of difference and same-ness' and how they have 'a major role in facilitating consideration of gender, race, and other axes of power in a wide range of political dis-cussions and academic disciplines' (Cho et al., 2013: 787). Ultimately, intersectionality is about power, it is about a way of isolating, studying and making visible inequalities that remain unseen because systems overly focus on one particular type of experience.

Arguments around universal basic income tend to overemphasize the experiences of women who might, to a certain extent, be included in aspects of society or, who live in capitalist societies where they have some or full participation in recognized patterns of employment and production. An intersectional approach to basic income could go beyond thinking of universal basic income as a way for the state to recognize the unpaid and unrecognized work of what women do in society without deepening inequalities further. Intersectionality could help the debate around a universal basic income go beyond the gender inequalities focused on employment patterns or labour-market representations for women. Instead it could help extend the debates into other intersections of disadvantage and exclusion, particularly highlighting the 'international nature of gender inequality' affecting women in the 'Global South' (McLean and McKay, 2015: 2), who live in and around abject poverty and conservative patriarchal societies.

Intersectionality opens up ways of thinking about the possible impact of a universal basic income on women's lives from a more, multilayered perspective of how varied women's lives can be. Such an approach aggregates meaning and complexity to the ideas of who women are, what women do, how women live and how the guarantee of a basic income can impact on women's lives. Intersectionality is also about diversifying the ways in which gender interacts with class, race, age, religion, geographical location and aspects of culture. To this effect, Cho et al. (2013: 785) argue that intersectionality interrogates the ways in which identities become intelligible and challenges the ways institutional and societal agendas tend to follow 'traditional single-axis horizons'. Without considering intersectionality some women's lives remain largely neglected in the literature, scholarship and policy formation around universal basic income. Studying and understanding the intersections of inequality which characterize particular circumstances around gender, race, class and age creates new productions of identity which can help bend and change how we advocate for a universal basic income for women more globally.

In Britain for example, there are multiple layers of inequalities for women, along the lines of not only gender, but also ethnicity, age and social class. Women from *black and minority ethnic groups* (BME) suffer from ethnic inequalities on top of, or in combination with, gendered inequality and discrimination. Many black women's employment experiences are not only shaped by economic factors, sexism and the sexual division of labour, but also racism too. It is 'the intersection between these elements that defines the distinct position of black women in the labour market as akin neither to that of white women nor to that of black men' (Lewis, 2017: 2). Racism describes the prejudiced and discriminatory organization of a society based on the ideological belief that there is inferiority grounded in 'race' or colour (biological differences) and/ or ethnic background (cultural differences). Black women in particular, face disproportionate levels of social inequality, because gender, race and social class all play a part in shaping black women's experiences. In Britain, many professions are still dominated by white, middle-class males. For instance, the work of lawyers, doctors, surgeons, senior managers and company chief executives are all predominantly male and white. When women are employed in these sectors, it is usually to carry out much lower paid, lower status work, such as nursing or caring work in the health sector, or secretarial and other administrative work in the law sector. BME women are less represented in the higher professions and are proportionately over-represented in the lower-paid, part-time and precarious occupations. One key question is: how might universal basic income change the experiences of BME women, in particular? On the one hand, a universal basic income could provide an important lifeline to women from black and ethnic minority groups. It can take women from BME groups out of poverty, providing a basic income to mitigate precarious and part-time work, and to rebalance the financial inequality women from BME groups have suffered over decades in Britain. On the other hand, while protecting women from *gross* poverty and inequality, a universal basic income could incentivize women to remain in the home, discouraging them to break the various glass ceilings which have prohibited women from BME groups achieving the opportunities and success of other social groups. From this perspective, a universal basic income can provide both pros and cons for women from BME groups.

Age is also a social category which intersects with gender (and other social categories). As women get older, both the private and public spheres of social life provide obstacles which affect this group of women in particular. For example, there has been a vast amount of feminist research dedicated to how *young women* experience sexism in contemporary society, particularly in the workplace (Morley, 1993; Savigny, 2014; Morley, 2014; Howe-Walsh and Turnbull, 2016). Many women who do become successful in the workplace, have had to fight against various forms of sexism to make it, only then to often have their careers 'disrupted' by having children and raising them. Unfortunately, in family breakdowns or separations, women are the ones who usually take prime responsibility of the young. To be clear, it is young women, not men, who become responsible for these family commitments. Most men are privileged enough not to suffer from these situations in the same way women do. The social inequalities of class, race and gender gets worse when an older woman stops paid work. Older women and those from BME groups are poorer than peer equivalents in middle age (Giddens and Sutton, 2013). The situation is exacerbated by the fact that women are less likely (than men) to have built-up considerable pensions for old age, thus the chances of having a private occupational or personal pension during working life, is a key determinant of income inequality among older people. A key question is: how might a universal basic income impact on women's pensions? There is little evidence of yet as to whether a universal basic income shall change the gendered inequalities of women in these various stages of the life course.

We have already seen how gender intersects with a number of other social influences – a woman's ethnicity; age, social status, and of course the country in which she is born. An important social category which intersects with all of these is *social class*. In India, for example, both men and women of different classes and castes must struggle to obtain and maintain equal rights, but women of all castes also have to fight against gender oppression. Women struggle against deep rooted attitudes and beliefs within the family, where girls and women are treated as inferior to boys and men, with most decision making and control is out of their reach. It is women, not men, who must 'struggle for equal rights, as individuals, within their households and wider families, and outside in various public spheres, including workplaces' (Devala et al., 2015: 160). In India, women (or girls) are married earlier than men, and have much fewer opportunities to participate in the labour force (Devala et al., 2015). Like most countries around the world, Indian society is deeply patriarchal, with most women having subordinate and inferior social status inside and outside of the home.

Overall, we can see that gender inequality is multifaceted and multilayered, with intersections of disadvantage traversing ethnicity, social class and age (among others) all playing an important part in the experiences of women. Universal basic income has the potential to counteract some of the economic in-balances women have experienced from being disadvantaged on a number of levels. But inequality is not only about economic relations, but also about a wider range of social conditions in which women are subjugated, exploited, disempowered and treated as second-class citizens. A universal basic income can argu-ably bring with it better values for all citizens (men and women), though also has some potential for harm, if encouraging and maintain-ing the traditional gendered division of labour as we currently know it – encouraging women to be in the home and men to dominate the public and most powerful positions in society. The notion of inter-sectionality has the potential to contribute to how we view the com-plexity of women's experience and allow for other analyses to emerge around the impact a universal basic income might have on women's lives.

Summary

This chapter introduced readers to the ways in which a universal basic income impacts on the work of women. Drawing on various feminist perspectives, this chapter showed that a universal basic income has the potential to increase women's autonomy, economic power and inde-pendence. While a universal basic income can empower women in many ways, from a feminist point of view it may not change current gender inequalities. While a universal basic income might contribute to the emancipation of women and possibly providing further economic freedom to women, freedom is complicated. If universal basic income, with its emphasis on individualism, might offer women an opportunity to act against traditional gender roles in society; this is not changing the normative ways in which people in our societies dictate gender relations.

Feminist thought and research explored around universal basic income shows how the introduction of this living stipend does not resolve the ongoing tensions between how women's role continues to evolve in society, amidst traditionalist and liberal or forward-looking views on the position of women. For example, a universal basic income might decrease the amount of women in the labour force and increase the likelihood that women will carry the domestic burden of unpaid care work (with women being tied more firmly, not less firmly, to the home). Through examining universal basic income it highlights how a gender-symmetry lifestyle may be undermined by a policy intended for good. Drawing on the notion of intersectionality, this chapter also explored some of the diverse and varied experiences of women, by looking at gender in relation to ethnicity, age, social class and the varied gendered experiences encountered by country and circumstance. It showed that a universal basic income can have varying effects on different social groups of women, in different places and throughout different stages of their lives.

References

Beem, C. (2005) 'Restoring the civic value of care in a post-welfare reform society'. In: L. M. Mead and C. Beem, eds. *Welfare Reform and Political Theory*. New York: Russell Sage Foundation.

Cho, S., Crenshaw, K. and McCall, L. (2013) 'Toward a field of intersectionality studies: Theory, applications and praxis'. *Signs: Journal of Women in Culture and Society*, 38(4), pp. 785–810.

Devala, S., Jhabvala, R., Mehta, S. K. and Standing, G. (2015) *Basic Income: A Transformative Policy for India*. London: Bloomsbury.

Dobrowolsky, A. (2010) 'Ruth Lister: Citizenship in theory and in practice'. *Women's Studies Quarterly*, 38(1/2), pp. 295–301.

Fraser, N. (1994) 'After the family wage: Gender equity and the welfare state'. *Political Theory*, 22(4), pp. 591–618.

Gheaus, A. (2008) 'Basic income, gender justice and costs of gender-symmetrical lifestyles'. *Basic Income Studies*, 3(3), pp. 1–8.

Giddens, A. and Sutton, P. W. (2013) *Sociology*. Cambridge: Polity Press.

Howe-Walsh, L. and Turnbull, S. (2016) 'Barriers to women leaders in academia: Tales from science and technology'. *Studies in Higher Education*, 41(3), pp. 415–428.

Lewis, G. (2017) 'Black women's employment and the British economy'. In: C. Harris and W. James, eds. *Inside Babylon: The Caribbean Diaspora in Britain*. London: Verso.

Lister, R. (2003) *Citizenship: Feminist Perspectives*, 2nd edition. London: Palgrave Macmillan.

McKay, A. (2005) *The Future of Social Security Policy: Women, Work and Citizens' Basic Income*. London: Routledge.

McLean, C. (2016) '... and justice for all? Basic income and the principles of gender equity'. *Juncture*, 22(4), 284–288.

McLean, C. (2015) *Beyond Care: Expanding the Feminist Debate on Universal Basic Income*. WiSE working paper no. 1. Glasgow: WiSE Research Centre.

McLean, C. and McKay, A. (2015) *Beyond Care: Expanding the Feminist Debate on Universal Basic Income*. Glasgow: WISE Research Centre. Retrieved from www.gcu.ac.uk/media/gcalwebv2/theuniversity/centresprojects/wise/90324WiSE_BriefingSheet.pdfMoller-Okin, S. (1991) *Justice, Gender and the Family*. New York: Basic Books.

Morley, L. (1993) 'Empowering women managers in the public sector'. *Women in Management Review*, 8(7), pp. 26–31.

Morley, L. (2014) 'Lost leaders: women in the global academy'. *Higher Education Research & Development*, 33(1), pp. 114–128.

Oakley, A. (1974) *Housewife*. London: Allen Lane.

O'Brien, P. (2017) *Universal Basic Income: Pennies from Heaven*. Stroud: The History Press.

Orloff, A. (2013) 'Why basic income does not promote gender equality'. In: K. Widerquist, J. A. Noguera, A. Y. Vanderborght and J. De Wispelaere, eds. *Basic Income: An Anthology of Contemporary Research*. London: Wiley-Blackwell.

Pateman, C. (2004) 'Democratizing citizenship: Some advantages of a basic income'. *Politics and Society*, 32(1), 89–105.

Robeyns I. (2010) 'Feminism, basic income and the welfare state'. In: C. Bauhardt and G. Çağlar, eds. *Gender and Economics*. VS Verlag für Sozialwissenschaften.

Savigny, H. (2014) 'Women, know your limits: Cultural sexism in academia'. *Gender and Education*, 26(7), pp. 794–809.

Schulz, P. (2017) 'Universal basic income in a feminist perspective and gender analysis'. *Global Social Policy*, 17(1), pp. 89–92.

Standing, G. (2017) *Basic Income: And How We Can Make it Happen*. London: Penguin.

Zelleke, A. (2011) 'Feminist political theory and the argument for an unconditional basic income'. *Policy and Politics*, 39(1), pp. 27–42.

6

UNIVERSAL BASIC INCOME AND SUSTAINABLE CONSUMPTION

Introduction

In this chapter, we examine some of the arguments on how a universal basic income can tackle climate change by helping to maintain ecological sustainability. We begin by mapping out what has become known as 'the Anthropocene', a term to denote how humans have become a new geological force, radically changing the natural environment in which we live. We show that the activities of humans are having a devastating impact on the planet, and drastic measures are needed to tackle global warming, combat pollution and rescue our ecosystems (Standing, 2019). Against the backdrop of the Anthropocene, we examine arguments that a universal basic income is good for sustainable consumption, by changing the consumerist mind-set linked to consumption and growth. We then make a case for creating a prosperous society without the need for growth (Jackson, 2017), by drawing on a universal basic income as a way to change the dynamics of work, which can have a positive impact on the natural environment. We show that it is possible to address involuntary unemployment without increases in productivity necessarily corresponding to growth in production (Van Parijs and Vanderborght, 2017). Drawing on Standing (2019) and others, this chapter also explores the use of eco-taxes as one way of changing environmental behaviours, as well as creating an additional pool of income which could help fund a universal basic income. Finally, this chapter discusses how environmental issues and the green agenda has gained political momentum in recent years, particularly among green parties, showing the implications this might have for moving towards a universal basic income.

The Anthropocene, climate change and sustainable consumption

Humans have produced enough concrete to cover the entire Earth's surface with a layer two millimetres thick, and have halved the population of trees from six trillion to three trillion since the beginning of agriculture. Levels of CO_2 have risen dramatically to the highest levels seen in at least 800,000 years, acidifying oceans and raising the Earth's temperature. Extinctions are running at an average of 1,000 times the typical rate before humans walked the Earth, with populations of fish, amphibians, reptiles, birds and mammals declining by 58% in the last forty years (Lewis and Maslin, 2018; Dean et al., 2014). These are consequences of the Anthropocene, the geological epoch where humans are dictating the future of the planet. The Anthropocene is a term that has been used to denote how humans have become a new geological force, or 'the current interval where humans have become a dominant force of global environmental change' (Dean et al, 2014: 276). It provides a term to describe the connection between how human activity changes and exploits nature. For example, an anthropocenic effect is that plastic has found itself in water in which people drink. Hence why environmental campaigners are calling for ways in which human activities can be changed or controlled, with universal basic income one policy option which has been at the forefront of green party politics for many years (Van Parijs and Vanderborght, 2017). This section discusses universal basic income against the backdrop of the Anthropocene, examining how an implementation of a basic income could help provide sustainable consumption and keep our economic growth in check for the sake of the environment.

Paul Crutzen and Eugene Stoermer were the first to call our time on Earth, the Anthropocene, with 'Anthropo-' denoting human and '-cene' denoting a geological period, documenting some of the changes to our environment and to ecosystems as created and accelerated by human activity (Crutzen and Stoermer, 2000). Crutzen and Stoermer (2000) provided an account of how *Homo sapiens* as a dominant species on Earth continue to alter geological systems and how 'humanity is responsible for a range of dangerous and simultaneous modifications to many crucial planetary systems parameters, as evidenced by data indicating that planetary boundaries have been crossed (Bińczyk, 2019: 2). Many of these changes and escalations affecting our environment have been linked to how human societies have been organized throughout history, such as, hunter-gatherer, agriculturist, mercantile capitalist, industrial capitalist and our current consumerist capitalist system (Lewis and Maslin, 2018). Each system has disrupted the balance of ecosystems and has led to greater exploitation of natural resources; with each system more energy and more human power are required. The most damaging and fast-paced changes have occurred very recently; for example, increases in population numbers, such as in the 'great acceleration' of the 1950s, when the world population doubled from 2.5 billion to 5 billion, benefit the current form of capitalism, which depends on work and consumerism (Dean et al., 2014: 277). But this acceleration in population, productivity and growth has proved to be damaging to the environment. In order to address the impact of the Anthropocene and reduce its effects on the environment, there has to be a slowdown in productive capitalism and the consumption associated with it (Bińczyk, 2019). As we shall see, universal basic income offers one possibility of helping to address these issues, by helping to change the growth mind-set and consumerist culture in which we live.

Our current patterns of work are problematic since they fuel consumerism by driving people towards materialism. Our hard work also drives production and profit which in turn, produces more waste and creates more demand for products globally which are polluting our planet (Lewis and Maslin, 2018). To disrupt this cyclical dynamic in which we work not just to survive but also to consume, sometimes needlessly, there must be a changed attitude to work and consumerism. A universal basic income can help by persuading us that we do not work so hard for the money we receive and it could contribute in diminishing our involvement in the productivity associated with work. Standing (2019: 23) claims that a universal basic income can help reduce the binary thinking that exists between 'work' and 'non-work' – work which is not 'paid labour' is unrecognized and invisible in society. To create a new way of living, a curb in the production of paid labour has to occur. Implementing a universal basic income would serve to recognize different forms of work and to stop the ever increasing growth that our system creates. A change of social policy is so vital to the environment that Standing (2019: 24) claims 'the onrushing ecological crisis may come to be regarded as the decisive justification for a basic income system'. A universal basic income is important because it has the potential to change the dynamic relations between work, the environment and consumer capitalism.

The acknowledgement of the Anthropocene and acceptance that radical change in human activity is required has at last become a key priority for global leaders. However, there has been far more rhetoric than affirmative action, to the dismay of environmental campaigners. In 2018, at the UN climate change summit in Poland, naturalist Sir David Attenborough gave a speech addressing delegates of almost two hundred nations. During his speech, he declared:

> Right now we are facing a manmade disaster of global scale, our greatest threat in thousands of years: climate change … If we don't take action, the collapse of our civilizations and the extinction of much of the natural world is on the horizon.
>
> *(Quoted in Carrington, 2018)*

The speech came against the backdrop of continued rising, manmade temperatures on Earth, as well as a context in which countries from around the world were expected to explain how they could meet the 2015 Paris climate deal. Three years prior to the summit in Poland, countries all over the world vowed to meet emission targets, cutting greenhouse gases and avoiding the most dangerous effects of climate change. The agreement involved setting a new goal of net zero emissions in the second half of the century, encouraging the transition away from fossil fuels and to a clean energy economy. Of course, the greenhouse gases of what most western nations consume is far greater than what they produce, because developed countries export their carbon emissions to developing countries where manufacturing and processing occurs (Druckman et al., 2007). So the agreement involves countries working together, to address a problem, and resolve an issue, that is one of the most important of the modern age. More recently, in April 2019, an environmental social movement called Extinction Rebellion carried out a protest movement, by occupying prominent sites of London, including Oxford Circus and Parliament Square. The protest was part of an ongoing campaign to raise awareness of imminent environmental threats which they called on the British government to address. The ongoing protests included campaigners chaining or gluing themselves to various places (including two protestors fixing themselves to the top of a train) with hundreds of protestors getting arrested by the British police. The protests raised awareness in the media and among the British public. It was no surprise then, that just weeks later in local UK elections, the Green Party gained an unprecedented number of seats on a record number of councils across Britain. Green parties across Europe also made substantial gain in the 2019 European Union elections. There is no coincidence that there is a move towards a greener agenda, while at the same time fresh calls for a universal basic income. The curb on growth and consumerist culture needs to take priority.

At present, in most societies around the world, people are exacerbating climate change because of the consumption levels and carbon footprints they produce in everything they do. The 'carbon footprint' describes the amount of carbon dioxide given off as a result of the activities of individuals in society. This includes emissions from driving a car, to flying on an airplane, to a whole range of consumerist behaviours. Changing behaviour can happen if governments implements new social policies, such as universal basic income, which in turn alters the kinds of behaviour and activities people involve themselves with. This might involve changing the dynamics of work, valuing 'work' which causes little or no ecological damage to our planet, such as caring for children or the elderly. But it can also involve implementing 'eco-taxes' (Standing, 2019) and/or changing the consumerist mind-set to a more ecological one (O'Brien, 2017). These are just some of the issues we discuss throughout the rest of this chapter.

Prosperity without growth: changing mind-sets and human behaviour

How might a universal basic income change the mind-set or perceptions of how we live our lives? And what impact might this have on the environment? Many believe that a universal basic income is 'greener' for society because it reduces the disruptive effect economic growth has on the natural environment (Offe, 2013; O'Brien, 2017). Part of this disruption relates to changing the perceptions of the way we live our lives. In his key text, *Prosperity Without Growth: Foundations for the Economy of Tomorrow*, Tim Jackson (2017) hones in on the values he believes are already inherent in people, which are not consumerist in nature. Bringing out this hidden potential in people can create a society which is better for everyone (and importantly, the planet) without the need to focus on economic growth:

> It's possible to eat better (or less) and exercise better (or more). It's possible to walk rather than ride. It's possible to own less stuff. It's possible to invest money more ethically. People do these things. For a variety of reasons. And sometimes they feel better for it. It's possible to breathe more deeply. To spend more time with our family and friends. To volunteer in the community. It's possible to be more creative. To be more charitable. To be kinder to each other. It's possible to engage in totally random acts of unwarranted kindness. People do all of these things. And strangely, all of them have been shown to have beneficial impacts on wellbeing. They cost nothing. They contribute nothing to the GDP. They have nothing to do with output or efficiency. They have everything to do with prosperity.
>
> *(Jackson 2017: 217)*

Providing an innovative outlook on prosperity, Jackson (2017) explains how it is possible to live in a world *without consumerism*, and how to live better by *consuming less*. It is precisely this vision of way of living which connects to principles of a universal basic income. For example, a basic income could potentially allow for people to spend more time with family and friends, or enable the time and space to volunteer in the community. But in addition to these things, the notion of a universal basic income provides a feeling of being valued by the community in which you live. Jackson (2017: 207) says that the current structure of incomes and wages is set up to consistently reward competitive, individualistic and materialistic outcomes, 'even when these are detrimental – as the lessons from the financial crisis made clear'. He adds that 'reducing the huge income disparities that result from this would send a powerful signal about what is valued in society' (Jackson, 2017: 207). Jackson argues for a society which has better recognition of those engaged in child care, care for the elderly or disabled, or in volunteer work, as this would help 'shift the balance of incentives away from status competition and towards a more co-operative, and potentially more altruistic, society'. Jackson (2017: 207) says that such a way 'could be facilitated by a citizen's [basic] income'. Arguing for a society which moves beyond the idea of 'growth', Jackson lays out a vision for a society which is ecologically sounder, but which can still have prosperity. To do this, he calls on the state for radical change, asking for new creative and imaginative policies to be implemented: 'Universal basic income, sovereign money, capital taxation, pension restructuring, fiduciary reform, financial prudence: these have all received increasing attention in the years since the financial crisis … They are ideas whose time has come' (Jackson, 2017: 221). A universal basic income is just one of the many suggestions Jackson puts forward here. But it is clear that universal basic income offers a very different approach to the environment, as the principles of universal basic income (see Chapter 2) offer the possibility of a world which is not always driven and underpinned by production, consumption and growth. Universal basic income offers one possible solution to what Jackson calls a 'post-growth' economy and what Seyfang (2011) says is part of 'new economics' – meeting our own needs without compromising future generations to meet theirs. Overall, the argument focuses on the idea that we need to develop new concepts of wealth and prosperity, allowing higher standards of living, less dependent on the Earth's finite resources (Seyfang, 2011).

Jackson (2017: 3) asks what prosperity can look like in a 'finite world', with 'limited resources' and 'a population expected to exceed ten billion people within a few decades'. He calls for a path towards a more sustainable and more equitable form of prosperity. He says that some simple logic shows us that industrial activity must at some point be bounded, adding that:

> Global economic output is now almost ten times bigger than it was in 1950. If it continues to expand at the same average rate – a prospect that economists and politicians almost universally hope for – the world economy in 2100 would be more than 20 times bigger than it is today: a staggering 200-fold increase in economic scale in the space of just a few generations.

> *(Jackson, 2017: 7)*

The effects of this expansion are unsustainable, since the resource use is limited by environmental constraints (Seyfang, 2011), thus societies must move towards more sustainable consumption patterns by changing the social dimension of economic activity. This is where universal basic income enters into the equation. Basic income is arguably a radical step towards changing mind-sets, shifting consumption patterns, and radically transforming lifestyles.

Fitzpatrick (2013) argues that universal basic income offers a means of slowing down economic growth and challenges the 'productivist' mind-set enshrined in contemporary culture. Indeed, one of the most important arguments for a universal basic income and a better environment is to use it as a way of changing the way people *think* about production, growth and development. After all, 'people are motivated by more than just simple economic gain' (Seyfang, 2011: xiii), and a universal basic income can help facilitate 'the development of a desirable (ecological) mindset' (O'Brien, 2017: 108) which could put an end to the 'rat-race' – an endless and self-defeating pursuit of growth and production which is characteristic of most western societies. O'Brien (2017: 108) says that a change in mind-set 'would help to facilitate the human and ecological potential opened up by the possibility of freedom from economic constraints'.

However, there are different perspectives on how to resolve these big questions on how to save the planet. For example, some debates ask whether countries should pursue 'anti-capitalist low consumption lifestyles' or instead, 'generate cleaner economic growth' (Seyfang, 2011:

3). Seyfang (2011: 1) says that 'shopping to save the planet is big business'. People do not need to constantly spend their money on 'flashy material goods such as cars or expensive watches', but instead may display status by 'spending money on experiences, music, travel, fair-trade foods, craft beers, artisan coffee, vintage bicycles, and vinyl collections'(O'Brien, 2017: 106–107). But for this to happen, there needs to be a broad shift towards the environment, and a realization that economic growth and the constant production of raw materials is not the be all and end all of our civilization.

Eco-taxes and universal basic income

Climate change, plastic pollution, fossil fuel energy, eco-taxes or green taxes can help discourage behaviour that damages the environment and contributes to global warming. Eco-taxes are also being used as a way to reduce the cost of living for people in other areas. The introduction of more eco-taxes is a policy gaining popularity globally. The European Union has been calling for a shift from taxing labour to taxing pollution, property and resource. This can encourage the reduction in the use of harmful resources and lead to a more resource-efficient economy (EEA, 2013). In recent years the European Union has seen a rise in revenues from eco-taxes, from €264 billion in 2002 to €369 billion in 2017 (Eurostat, 2018). Nevertheless, these tax measures are still highly unused, only amounting to 0.08% of the gross domestic product (GDP) in the EU, despite an increasing desire to move taxation away from labour and more towards pursuing a greener agenda (EEA, 2018).

Like many advocates of the policy, Standing (2019) sees universal basic income as one approach to help tackle global warming. Eco-taxes which are then distributed to the population are also seen as having other effects which can help create a more egalitarian society. Taxing high environmental impact and CO_2 emissions has been discussed as producing a circular economy, where producers are motivated to invest in renewable energy and consumers are rewarded from consuming greener energy (Böhringer and Müller, 2014). There are several ways of achieving this with universal basic income. For example, one solution put forward by Standing (2019) is to have a 'Canadian-Swiss' model, which involves creating 'eco-taxes' on fuel and other high emissions activities, with those dividends distributed to others in a basic income, something which both Canada and Switzerland appear to be moving towards with the eco-taxes they have in place.

In Canada, the government passed a carbon tax which is aimed at giving Canadians more money. Under the Greenhouse Gas Pollution Pricing Act the Canadian government implemented a revenue-neutral carbon tax. The act states that, 'there is broad scientific consensus that anthropogenic greenhouse gas emissions contribute to global climate change' with the objective of stabilizing 'greenhouse gas concentrations in the atmosphere at a level that would prevent dangerous anthropogenic interference with the climate system' (ECCC, 2019). The act follows the precedent of the Paris climate agreement of 2015, aiming to reduce or limit global warming to less than two degrees Celsius above pre-industrial temperatures. To meet these requirements Canada's carbon tax is important on both a national and international level. However, unlike other countries, Canada took the steps to reduce carbon emissions while also reducing poverty in society – with all of the taxed monies redistributed to the provinces from which they were generated. The provinces then rebate about 90% of the revenues back to individual tax payers. The rebates are expected to exceed the increased energy costs for about 70% of Canadian households. For example:

> A Manitoba family will receive $336 rebate in 2019 compared to its increased costs of $232. A similar family in Saskatchewan will receive $598 compared with its higher costs of $403. In Ontario families will receive $300 to offset its $244 in carbon taxes and in New Brunswick a $248 rebate will more than offsets the average household costs of $202. The rebates will more than double by 2022 as the carbon tax rises, and the net financial benefit to household will grow over time.
>
> *(Nuccitelli, 2018)*

The Canadian approach to eco-taxes involves redistributing money directly back to households, showing how tax systems can be used to help the environment as well as supporting families.

Switzerland is also currently undergoing a massive restructuring of its energy system. One of the main reasons for this is Switzerland's ambitious environmental target of cutting domestic CO_2 emissions per-capita emissions from 5.8 tons in 2012 to 1.5 tons in 2050. Switzerland is effectively trying to transition to a low-carbon economy without a nuclear option. Switzerland has decided to withdraw from the use of nuclear energy within the next decades on a step-by-step basis: The existing five nuclear power plants are to be decommissioned when they reach the end of their safe service life, and will not be replaced by new ones (Böhringer and Müller, 2014: 1). Along with these changes Switzerland has also introduced measures such as taxing carbon in order to steadily decarbonize their economy. But importantly, it is how these taxes are used in Switzerland which is of interest to the topic of universal basic income. The Swiss government are redistributing taxes to those who are the worse-off in society – a policy action which has resonance with universal basic income.

Standing (2019) claims that eco-taxes would be a realistic way to fund a universal basic income and advantageous for three reasons. First, he believes that it would be an *effective* way of combating environmental concerns in the way that Canada and Switzerland do. Second, he believes that this system is *redistributive*, as it helps to pass the tax back to people who require it. Third, he believes it will be *popular*, as it appears to be in Switzerland (Standing, 2019). But this is highly controversial, since eco-taxes are notorious for hitting the poorest in society the hardest, as highlighted by the *gilets jaunes* (yellow vest) fuel tax protests in France, 2019. President Macron's flat tax on motor fuel was seen by some as an attack on the poorest in society, since the tax would eat up disposable income and worse affected those who lived in rural and suburban areas, with poor accessibility to good public transport (an argument which is also taken up in Chapter 7). However, Macron's policy was to fuel tax people struggling to make ends meet while diverting the proceeds to build wind farms, while the eco-tax Standing (2019) advocates for, is aimed at using the proceeds to fund a universal basic income. But this is just one practical way in which a universal basic income can help tackle environmental concerns – there are others too.

Arguments around eco-taxes are almost always seen as unpopular because companies and industry do not want to have their profits curtailed. Renewable energies are expensive both for the producers and for the consumers, further highlighting the importance of devising ways to redistribute wealth. Such a measure could very realistically be the introduction of a universal basic income. Furthermore, if we are to try and counteract the impact we have on the environment, we need to compromise beyond measures such as, recycling, by also changing the way in which we produce energy and products, and how we consume these products. Implementing eco-taxes in a more uniform way can create an economic and social and cultural environment where the waste of fossil fuels is seen as unattractive.

Moving towards a green agenda

Finally, we ask, in what ways is politics moving towards a green agenda? Many political groups believe that a universal basic income is good for the planet because its philosophy critiques the idea that societies must constantly maximize production in order to be successful. Green parties across different countries are strong advocates of a universal basic income because it has a green agenda. Some of the reasons Green-Party doctrine aligns itself with a universal basic income are partly to do with how Green parties recognize society's need to 'reduce their expectations regarding the growth of material standards of living' (Van Parijs and Vanderborght, 2017: 201). The introduction of a universal basic income, enough to cover basic needs, might entice people to go for less lucrative jobs. This attracts the interest of those in Green Parties because it puts less importance on the consumption of material goods and greater importance 'to the enjoyment of pleasurable work and leisure' (Van Parijs and Vanderborght, 2017: 201). Thus environmental constraints should be the basis for how we think about production and consumption, so a policy levelling the earning potential of whole populations, should have positive effects on the development of consumer capitalism (Lewis and Maslin, 2018). Jackson (2017: 113) refers to how we have become a 'throwaway society', a process which hurts the environment through the unnecessary accumulation of goods, a process worsened by the accumulation of wealth.

Another important reason for Green Parties to support a universal basic income comes in the form of a basic proposition, 'that nature and its resources are the common heritage of humankind' (Van Parijs and Vanderborght, 2017: 201). Following this premise Green Parties believe that those companies and individuals who benefit and profit from the consumption and refinement of raw materials on Earth and which pollute at accelerated rates, should pay into a fund to be distributed to all, unconditionally. Such views reflect how we are all deserving to enjoy the benefits of the profits drawn from exploiting natural resources, regardless of whether we have worked or laboured for them, we are all entitled to these. Therefore, a universal basic income is a measure to address the major inequalities that have arisen with accelerated economic growth and mass unemployment and precarious work.

Lastly, the policies behind the Green movement have attempted to decelerate growth but without increasing the problem of mass unemployment. One way of preventing the problem of mass unemployment, while also reducing productivity and growth, is to change the dynamics of work arrangements in society, as Van Parijs and Vanderborght explain:

> By turning some employment into voluntary unemployment and thereby sharing the existing jobs among more people, it makes it possible to address involuntary unemployment without productivity increases needing to be constantly translated into a corresponding growth in production.
>
> *(Van Parijs and Vanderborght, 2017: 201)*

A universal basic income has been viewed as a way to facilitate green lifestyles, because it has the potential to reduce the use of natural and human resources. Green advocates of a universal basic income believe that the point of economic development should not be focused on maximizing consumption, since this is ultimately bad for the environment and the future of the planet. For many Green party activists, a universal basic income can be 'a way of reconciling the environmental objective of taming growth with the social objective of reducing unemployment' (Van Parijs and Vanderborght, 2017: 202). A universal basic income provides an alternative to this premise pursued by Green parties, namely, basic income 'dissociates income from productive contribution, an unconditional basic income can be viewed as a systemic curb on growth' (Van Parijs and Vanderborght, 2017: 201). The problem of growth is one which concerns the Green movement because upholding the need to protect the environment also requires not just a different type of politics, but also a different type of economics. A change from an economy which is enormously productive, to one which is prosperous but not so focused on consumption and materialism as a way of life. Referring to this idea, Jackson asserts, 'the task of the economy is to deliver and to enable prosperity. But prosperity is not synonymous with material wealth and its requirements go beyond material sustenance' (Jackson, 2017: 121). A universal basic income can work as a way to diminish the productivity associated with employment, which in turn boosts material growth, consumption and wastage capitalism.

All over the globe, Green parties have been putting universal basic income at the top of their agendas. In the US, for example, the Green Party has continually incorporated basic income in all of its electoral platforms. In the 2014 platform, they stated:

> We call for a universal basic income (sometimes called a guaranteed income, negative income tax, citizen's income or citizen dividend). This would go to every adult regardless of health, employment, or marital status, in order to minimize government bureaucracy and intrusiveness into people's lives. The amount should be sufficient so that anyone who is unemployed can afford basic food and shelter. State or local governments should supplement that amount from local revenues where the cost of living is high.
>
> *(Cited in Van Parijs and Vanderborght, 2017: 198)*

Calls for a universal basic income by green parties are commonplace all over the world. Germany's Green Party, 'Die Grunen' (The Greens) hosted BIEN's eighth basic income congress in 2000 and have continued to support the idea of a universal basic income. The French green party, 'Europe Ecologie Les Verts' (Europe Ecology the Greens) have also been pressing for a 'citizen's income' or steps towards it. In 2013, 70% of its affiliates voted in favour of a motion supporting the introduction of a basic income in France (Van Parijs and Vanderborght, 2017: 200). In the Netherlands, the main green party, GroenLinks (Green Left) have also been pressing for basic income experiments to take place across the country. Plans were put together for a basic income trial in *Utrecht*, one of the largest cities in the Netherlands, (along with nineteen other Dutch municipalities) which would see claimants receiving more than six hundred euros per month. But plans for the experiments have been slow to move forward. In 'austere times', the term 'basic income' came across as politically toxic with several politicians (expected to implement the trial) deleting the term 'basic income' from the policy documents altogether. 'We had to delete mention of basic income from all the documents to get the policy signed off by the council', confided Lisa Westerveld, a Green councillor for the city of Nijmegen, near the Dutch–German border (Boffey, 2015). There is much scepticism about the scheme, as some Dutch citizens believed in the common myth, that a basic income could encourage idleness. Some are worried that it is 'just free money and people will sit at home and watch TV', said Heleen de Boer, a Green councillor in the city (Guardian, 2017). As a consequence of these political and public debates, the scale of the experiments shrunk and did not go ahead as expected.

The Green Party in the UK also supports the idea of a basic income and has called for further research into the different models of basic income in the House of Commons. Recently in the UK the Scottish Green Party has also referred to a possible citizen's income, payable to everyone to meet their basic needs. A recent report by Standing (2019), *Basic Income as Common Dividends: Piloting a Transformative Policy*, which was presented to the shadow chancellor of the exchequer, John McDonnell, has also articulated a possible outline of how a basic income could be implemented in the UK. All of these developments, which are strongly endorsed by Green parties, keep alive the idea of a basic income in UK politics.

There are, as explored in this section, current political trends which support a universal basic income as a policy to create different dynamics of living in societies which have become highly unequal. The political agendas of green parties are particularly supportive of the introduction a universal basic income and this goes hand in hand with increased taxation on energy, pollution and resources. Green parties recognize that to create a system where eco-taxes rise requires the consumer to pay more for services. Therefore, a basic income helps alleviate the rise in pricing which could occur if, for example, we moved to more renewable energy sources. A universal basic income appears as tightly linked with the type of politics which seek to create change by broadening the taxation system and changing the way in which funds are redistributed to the general public.

Summary

This chapter focused on exploring ecological futures and the implications for a universal basic income. First, this chapter introduced the notion of the Anthropocene and an overview of how changes to the environment are directly linked to human activity and the way we live in a capitalist society. Second, this chapter presented some critical explorations which have been put forward by different authors in order to reduce our impact on the planet's ecosystems, and how adopting a universal basic income has arisen as a possibility. There are good arguments as to how a universal basic income can help 'reduce or avoid the human activities which are causing climate change' (Seyfang, 2011: xii), but there are others which have been discussed in this chapter, such as, economic prosperity without growth, changing our attitude to consumerism and the political agendas of Green parties. Some of the key points included changing our perceptions of consumerism, production and growth, while also examining how universal basic income could help support employment without necessarily increasing forms of production and growth. Moreover, this chapter also discussed how the political agenda must become 'greener'. We showed and described how that there is a surge of green campaigners and green parties pursuing universal basic income, as one way to help tackle the ecological issues we are all faced with, but we also showed that the state must radically shift its focus away from growth. Universal basic income is one possible solution to help with this shift.

Another important suggestion around universal basic income discussed in the chapter was eco-taxes as a means to tackle the effects of global warming. The chapter illustrated how there are countries, such as Canada and Switzerland, where carbon emissions are taxed in order to help their economies to become decarbonized. Eco-taxes could be a way to meet environmental targets set to be met in the next three decades to come. Yet, there are also some considerations to be taken into account, since taxes on fossil fuels very often hit the poorest first and more significantly. Thus, a redistribution scheme which could be delivered through a universal basic income is discussed as a way to tackle poverty and provide some extra financial support to families. Eco-taxes as a measure have been discussed as a way to help fund the policy of a universal basic income. The examples elaborated on show how the taxing of carbon emissions might help industries seek new alternatives to fossil fuels and can encourage people to live more environmentally friendly lives.

The adverse climate effects brought on by human activity and the question over the future of the planet is probably one of the most important issues humanity has faced, if not *the* most important issue. There has to be 'considerable economic and social adaptation to the impacts of climate change' (Seyfang, 2011: xii) ensuring that economic growth and resource consumption is compatible with environmental sustainability. The problems of 'excess nutrient loading, species loss, ocean acidification and climate change already represent a serious threat to the integrity of ecological systems' and 'threaten to undermine the foundations for human society' (Jackson, 2017: 17). Universal basic income will not eradicate these problems. It only offers some practical solutions for changing our approach to growth and help with the prospect of 'living lightly on the planet' (Maniates, 2002: 47). It may help reduce consumption but it is impossible to remove all forms of consumption since 'we only achieve a zero-consumption lifestyle when we are dead' (Seyfang, 2011: 5). Most advocates for a universal basic income believe that it can have a positive impact on the natural environment. But it may not be the only solution.

References

Bińczyk, E. (2019) 'The most unique discussion of the 21st century? The debate on the Anthropocene pictured in seven points'. *The Anthropocene Review*, 6(1–2), pp. 3–18.

Boffey, D. (2015) 'Dutch city plans to pay citizens a "basic income", and Greens say it could work in the UK'. *The Guardian*, 26 December. Retrieved from www.theguardian.com/world/2015/dec/26/dutch-city-utrecht-basic-income-uk-greens

Böhringer, C. and Müller, A. (2014) 'Environmental tax reforms in Switzerland: A computable general equilibrium impact analysis'. *Swiss Society of Economics and Statistics*, 150(1), pp. 1–21.

Carrington, D. (2018) 'David Attenborough: Collapse of civilisation is on the horizon'. *The Guardian*, 3 December. Retrieved from www.theguardian.com/environment/2018/dec/03/david-attenborough-collapse-civilisation-on-horizon-un-climate-summit

Crutzen, P. J. and Stoermer, E. F. (2000) 'The Anthropocene'. *Global Change Newsletter*, 41, pp. 17–18.

Dean, J., Leng, M. and Mackay, A. (2014) 'Is there an isotopic signature of the Anthropocene?'. *The Anthropocene Review*, 1(3), pp. 276–287.

Druckman, A.Bradley, P.Papathanasopoulou, E. and Jackson, T. (2007) 'Measuring progress towards carbon reduction in the UK'. *Ecological Economics*, 66 (4), pp. 594–604.

EEA (2013) 'Green fiscal reform can create jobs and stimulate innovation in the EU'. Retrieved on 28 May 2019 from www.eea.europa.eu/highlights/fiscal-reform-can-create-jobs

EEA (2018) 'Environmental and labour taxation'. Retrieved on 28 May 2019 from www.eea.europa.eu/airs/2018/resource-efficiency-and-low-carbon-economy/environmental-and-labour-taxation

ECCC (2019) 'Environment and climate change Canada'. Retrieved on 28 May 2019 from www.canada.ca/en/revenue-agency/campaigns/pollution-pricing.html

Eurostat (2018) 'Statistics explained – environmental tax statistics'. Retrieved on 28 May 2019 from https://ec.europa.eu/eurostat/statistics-explained/index.php/Environmental_tax_statistics

Fitzpatrick, T. (2013) 'Ecologism and basic income'. In: K. Widerquist, J. A. Noguera, Y. Vanderborght and J. de Wispelaere, eds. *Basic Income: An Anthology of Contemporary Research*. Chichester: Wiley Blackwell.

Jackson, T. (2017) *Prosperity Without Growth: Foundations for the Economy of Tomorrow*. New York: Routledge.

Lewis, S. L. and Maslin, M. A. (2018) *The Human Planet: How We Created the Anthropocene*. London: Penguin Books.

Maniates, M. (2002) 'Individualisation: Plant a tree, buy a bike, save a world?'. In: T. Princen, M. Maniates and K. Konka, eds. *Confronting Consumption*. Cambridge, MA: MIT Press.

Nuccitelli, D. (2018) 'Canada passed a carbon tax that will give most Canadians more money'. *The Guardian*, 26 October. Retrieved from www.theguardian.

com/environment/climate-consensus-97-per-cent/2018/oct/26/canada-pa
ssed-a-carbon-tax-that-will-give-most-canadians-more-money

O'Brien, P. (2017) *Basic Income: Pennies from Heaven*. Stroud: The History Press.

Offe, C. (2013) 'A non-productivist design for social policies'. In: K. Widerquist, J. A. Noguera, Y. Vanderborght and J. de Wispelaere, eds. *Basic
Income: An Anthology of Contemporary Research*. Chichester: Wiley Blackwell.

Seyfang, G. (2011) *The New Economics of Sustainable Consumption*. Basingstoke:
Palgrave Macmillan.

Standing, G. (2019) *Basic Income as Common Dividends: Piloting a Transformative
Policy*. London: Progressive Economy Forum.

Van Parijs, P. and Vanderborght, Y. (2017) *Basic Income: A Radical Proposal for a
Free Society and a Sane Economy*. Cambridge, MA: Harvard University Press.

7

AGAINST A UNIVERSAL BASIC INCOME

Introduction

This chapter presents arguments against a universal basic income by examining some of the key criticisms and outlining the potential problems associated with its implementation. While the majority of studies within academic literature have focused on what is positive about a basic income policy, there is much less academic literature written on what are the drawbacks and difficulties with such a reform, leaving the basic income debate rather one-sided. We begin examining arguments against, by looking at the problems of cost and affordability, 'welfare dependency' and reliance on the welfare state. We then outline some problems with universal basic income, by turning to a range of alternatives, such as endowment or stake-holding policies (see Ackerman and Alstott, 1999) or plans for an 'annual cash grant' (see Murray, 2006). Within this discussion, we also examine different variations of a universal basic income, with some advocates pushing forward a neoliberal case for a basic income (Bowman, 2013) and ask whether or not universal basic income would work out if designed and implemented under various right-wing governments. Later in this chapter, we return to some issues raised in previous chapters, by looking at the adverse effects a universal basic income might have on women, particularly in relation to the 'sexual division of labour'. We also look at the effects a universal basic income might have on migration, migrant workers and perceptions of citizenship and rights to a universal basic income.

In most texts on universal basic income, against arguments *rarely* feature, usually because authors writing the text are pushing for its implementation. With this in mind, we believe that this chapter shall provide a number of refreshing perspectives on the downsides and alternatives to a universal basic income.

Cost, affordability and the side-effects of heavier taxes

There are some 'usual suspects' which come to mind when discussing arguments *against* a universal basic income. These are arguments which are highlighted by politicians, journalists, political commentators, and some social scientists. Some of these arguments are based on *solid facts* and worthwhile evidence, but some are based on *fiction* or myth. Here we try to disentangle fact from fiction and examine which of these provide good arguments against a universal basic income. We begin by looking at the cost and affordability of a universal basic income. John Kay, former director of the Institute for Fiscal Studies (UK), says: 'If you do the numbers, either the basic income is unrealistically low or the tax rate to finance it is unacceptably high. End of story' (Guardian, 2019). Crudely calculated, implementing a universal basic income in Britain, where the state would give everyone 20% of the average income – about £120 per week – would mean raising £400 billion a year. Critics of a universal basic income say that this is equivalent to inventing new taxes that raise as much as the combined revenues of income tax, national insurance and corporation tax. For example, Professor Ian Goldin, from Oxford University, says that universal basic income is 'financially irresponsible'; even in the richest societies, 'if [universal basic income] was set at a level to provide a modest but decent standard of living it would be unaffordable and lead to ballooning deficits' (Goldin, 2018).

As with any welfare or policy reform, the cost and affordability of the scheme must be taken into account, as a failure to fund the plan would kill dead a universal basic income from the offset. Advocates for a universal basic income argue that it could be funded in a variety of ways, from raising income tax, to implementing a wealth tax and closing tax havens (Parncutt, 2012) or using dividends from an eco-tax (Standing, 2019). The problems with these tax methods are the side-effects they create. For example, an eco-tax might be good for the environment (see Chapter 6), but it would be deeply unpopular with the public, and could hit some of the poorest people the hardest. This was the case in France, where President Macron had to re-think green taxes, after the yellow vest fuel tax protests of 2019. When a government imposes a flat tax on motor fuel, as Macron did, it usually hits poorest people hardest as it eats up their disposable income. However, re-directing carbon taxes to help the worse-off is one way of using an eco-tax, as Standing (2019) and others have argued. As we can see, raising money using eco-taxes to fund a universal basic income is a controversial issue. Likewise, a wealth tax (a levy on the total value of personal assets) will have the undesired effect of influencing where wealthy people reside, with many moving wealth abroad, or pushing investment to other parts of the world. Until recently, France had a wealth tax known as the *solidarity tax on wealth*, or ISF (*impôt de solidarité sur la fortune*). The tax was initiated in 1982 under François Mitterrand, but was abandoned only recently, in light of wealthy families fleeing to other parts of Europe where their wealth is 'better looked after'. In the context of Brexit, France see dropping their wealth tax as a way of attracting wealthy individuals from Britain to France, whose investment and spending powers can boost the local economy. In the US, Democrat Senator Elizabeth Warren proposed a 2% wealth tax on the family's net worth over $50 million with an extra 1% on net worth greater than $1 billion (Stevens, 2019). On the one hand, this appears to be a good solution to resourcing the US State purse. On the other hand, a wealth tax can result in driving wealthy tax payers elsewhere – with the US State purse ultimately losing out.

Creating a culture of dependency: reliance on the welfare state

Ian Goldin (2018) says that we need to 'radically change the way we think about income and work', but we must 'forget about universal basic income'. A universal basic income merely postpones a more important discussion for political and corporate leaders to talk about the future of jobs. What we need is 'more part-time work, shorter weeks, and rewards for home work, creative industries and social and individual care' (Goldin, 2018). Goldin argues that universal basic income is a 'red herring' – it distracts us to how to solve problems with unemployment and poverty. He writes:

> Universal basic income will undermine social cohesion. Individuals gain not only income, but meaning, status, skills, networks and friendships through work. Delinking income and work, while rewarding people for staying at home, is what lies behind social decay. Crime, drugs, broken families and other socially destructive outcomes are more likely in places with high unemployment, as is evident in the drug pandemic in the US.
>
> *(Goldin, 2018)*

Goldin (2018) also argues that universal basic income undermines incentives to participate in society. A universal basic income provides a 'guarantee of a lifetime of dependence' (Goldin, 2018) not the means required to help people overcome unemployment and find work, or retrain in order to build new employment skills. Goldin (2018) believes that 'stronger safety nets' are needed to provide a 'lifeline towards meaningful work and participation in society'. Goldin's arguments are not without evidence. There is a whole history around the idea that state welfare provision creates a *culture of dependency* since the 1970s and earlier. The American sociologist and New Right theorist Charles Murray (1984) observed the consequences of 'state dependency', laid out in his work *Losing Ground: American Social Policy 1950–1980*. In this key text, Murray (1984) argued that welfare provisions implemented in the United States tended to increase poverty rather than decrease it, because they provided incentives to reward short-term goals, but not to escaping poverty in the long-term. Since the 1980s, Murray has used the term 'underclass' to describe 'a class of people who exist at the margins of American society', who are 'usually poor' and live in a community of illegitimacy, crime and labour force drop-out (Murray, 2006: 61). The underclass described the worst of social conditions, including poor parental supervision; disaffected youth; mass unemployment; single-parent households, and a general isolation from mainstream patterns and norms. These 'outcast' communities where the underclass can be found are all too familiar in urban and city areas across Europe, the US, and the rest of the world. Murray (1984) argued that the underclass was a by-product of poor welfare policies, a toxic culture which was made worse, not better, by state welfare programs. This set of ideas, also known as 'welfare dependency', is very persuasive in understanding how whole communities become reliant upon handouts from the State and how it can discourage people from entering the world of work.

A universal basic income can encourage welfare dependency because there is no 'need' to work. In this sense, a universal basic income undermines incentives to participate in society (Goldin, 2018). A universal basic income discourages individuals and families from participating in society, leading to a culture of idleness, rather than providing the means with which people can learn a new skill, retrain, or move city in order to find work. It incentivizes people to be stagnant rather than to create change. Searching for a job already requires a great deal of motivation and will power (Altman et al., 2017) and a universal basic income could make people less motivated and over-reliant on the funds received from the State.

Some commentators on universal basic income argue that it can be parasitic. A parasite is an organism which lives in or on another organism, deriving nutrients or other benefits from it, at its host's expense. In his work *The Right to Exploit: Parasitism, Scarcity, Basic Income*, Van Donselaar (2009: 4) describes a parasitic relation existing between two parties (A and B) whereby 'A is worse off than she would have been had B not existed or if she would have had nothing to do with him, while B is better off than he would have been without A, or having nothing to do with her, or vice versa.' The tapeworm in a dog's stomach is better-off and the dog is worse-off having come into contact with each other. Some recipients of a universal basic income are arguably parasitic because they derive income from the work of others – their host. This argument, known as parasitism, becomes particularly applicable to those who are considered as too lazy to work. Van Donselaar (2009) argues that a universal basic income is parasitic because it does not discriminate between those who are poor due to bad luck and those who are poor because they are unwilling to work. Here, Van Donselaar (2009) seemingly distinguishes between those who have been dealt a bad hand, perhaps born into a set of poor circumstances and those who have opportunities to work but prefer to 'sponge off' others. It can be argued that a universal basic income will encourage parasitism – a culture in which members of society become reliant on others to work and generate income.

Different kinds of universal basic income and some of the alternatives

Universal basic income is not the only policy on offer. So what are the *alternatives?* Some have argued for a one-off endowment, given to citizens at the start of adult life. For example, in *The Stakeholder Society*, Ackerman and Alstott (1999: 3) offer a 'practical plan for reaffirming the reality of a common citizenship' by suggesting that 'as each American reaches maturity, he or she will be guaranteed a stake of eighty thousand dollars' (Ackerman and Alstott, 1999: 3). In their view, their plan 'seeks justice by rooting it in capitalism's preeminent value: the importance of private property' (Ackerman and Alstott, 1999: 3). Every citizen can use the US$80,000 for whatever purpose they choose: 'to start a business or pay for more education, to buy a house or raise a family or save for the future' (Ackerman and Alstott, 1999: 5). There is however, one important clause in Ackerman and Alstott's plan, since every stakeholder has a 'special responsibility' to repay the eighty thousand dollars back into the stake-holding fund at death.

Giving young adults a start-up fund of eighty thousand dollars provides a number of opportunities which they could not have ordinarily have access to, as Ackerman and Alstott point out:

> Stakeholding liberates college graduates from the burdens of debt, often with something to spare. It offers unprecedented opportunities for the tens of millions who don't go to college and have often been shortchanged by their high school educations. For the first time, they will confront the labor market with a certain sense of security. The stake will give them the independence to choose

where to live, whether to marry, and how to train for economic opportunity. Some will fail. But fewer than today.

(Ackerman and Alstott, 1999: 5)

The 'stakeholder idea' is different to a universal basic income, but still very appealing to politicians and the public. Rather than focusing on 'decency' and 'minimum provision' as some argue a basic income provides, the 'stakeholder idea' wants to maximize success and opportunity. It does not prioritize 'safety nets' as a universal basic income does, but instead looks at 'starting points' for opportunity and a more successful way of living (Ackerman and Alstott, 1999: 8). Such an idea is not about 'welfare reform' but 'an entirely new enterprise' which maps out a plan for 'economic citizenship' (Ackerman and Alstott, 1999: 8). The basis for a stake-holding fund resonates with a universal basic income, insofar as it is based on the values of freedom and equal opportunity, and that it can provide a 'certain sense of security' (see the extract above). Advocates of a basic income, however, argue that a universal basic income is better, because it provides regular payments rather than a one-off, avoiding the chances of people recklessly blowing their funds all in one go. But here the idea of 'freedom' is raised once more, since advocates of endowment or stakeholder funds perceive a basic income as being more tightly controlled by the State. Whereas, with an upfront cash fund, people have the freedom to blow it all if they wish. Ackerman and Alstott say this:

In a free society, it is inevitable that different stakeholders will put their resources to different uses, with different results. Our goal is to transcend the welfare state mentality, which sets conditions on the receipt of 'aid'. In a stakeholding society, stakes are a matter of right, not a handout. The diversity of individuals' life choices (and the predicable failure of some) is no excuse for depriving each American of the wherewithal to attempt her own pursuit of happiness.

(Ackerman and Alstott, 1999: 8–9)

Here, Ackerman and Alstott stress a number of points which has resonance with a universal basic income – like putting resources to different uses; removing the 'conditions' on the receipt of 'aid'; providing a 'right' to citizens, rather than a handout. In addition to these benefits, they argue that individuals should have the freedom to fail, if they so wish.

Apart from there being alternatives to a universal basic income, there are also *different versions* of a universal basic income, some which come from both the left and right of politics. In May 2019, Guy Standing published his report *Basic Income as Common Dividends: Piloting a Transformative Policy*, which was prepared for the shadow chancellor of the exchequer. Just days later, the shadow chancellor, John McDonnell, announced that universal basic income pilots will be included in Labour's next election manifesto. More than ever before, Britain's political *left* is looking closely at the prospect of a universal basic income, by putting ideas for a basic income into policy. But a universal basic income is supported by some of those on the *right* of the political spectrum too. For example, the executive director of the Adam Smith Institute, Sam Bowman (2013), says that 'The *ideal welfare system is a basic income*, replacing the existing anti-poverty programmes the government carries out' (cited in O'Hagan, 2017: 1; emphasis added). Highlighting Milton Friedman's (1962) proposal for a negative income tax, Bowman (2013) provides a 'neoliberal case for a basic income', by arguing that it would (1) address in-work poverty, (2) reduce complexity in the welfare system, and (3) facilitate other reforms that would raise overall living standards. Bearing these examples in mind, we see that proposals for a universal basic income cut right across the political spectrum, with advocates for the policy coming from all walks of political life. But surely this would provide different versions of a universal basic income? And might it provide a version of basic income with differential principles and values? Some commentators believe that a neoliberal case for a universal basic income would see it rolled out as a distinctly right-wing initiative (O'Hagan, 2017), with a prime focus on dismantling, or shrinking the welfare state, as well as forgetting about the needs of the most vulnerable in society altogether. Indeed, when Bowman (2013: 1) alludes to a basic income, 'or something like it', he sees it as a way of fixing the current welfare state.

Another alternative to a universal basic income is laid out in Charles Murray's (2006) text, *In Our Hands: A Plan to Replace the Welfare State*.

Here, Murray proposes a plan that sees everyone over the age of twenty-one (in the US) receive an annual cash grant of $10,000, with a surtax, 'funded by eliminating the transfers that currently exist' (Murray, 2006: 14). Some of Murray's (2006) premises are not too dissimilar from those advocating for a basic income, saying that: 'Here's the money. Use it as you see fit. Your life is in your hands' (Murray, 2006: 14). Murray's plan for an annual cash grant has many similarities with a universal basic income (i.e. it is universal and has 'no strings attached'). But what are Murray's reasons for implementing such a policy? And how might his reasons affect the ways in which the policy is implemented? Murray certainly believes that the current welfare state is detrimental to society and wants to replace it. He says:

> The welfare state produces its own destruction. The process takes decades to play out, but it is inexorable. First, the welfare state degrades the traditions of work, thrift, and neighborliness that enabled a society to work at the outset; then it spawns social and economic problems that it is powerless to solve. The welfare state as we have come to know it is everywhere within decades of financial and social bankruptcy.
>
> *(Murray, 2006: 3–4)*

For Murray, it is crucial to replace the current welfare system with a cash payment that can provide an annual cash grant to every citizen. Murray's proposal is different to a universal basic income, though there are some common ideas, based on a universal way of redistributing wealth to citizens. Most commentators agree that the welfare state has to change form, but there are clearly different proposals to how this might happen, and universal basic income is merely one of them.

Reinforcing the sexual division of labour

On the one hand, a universal basic income can be seen as a way of emancipating women, by providing them with an income for care and domestic work which they have always had to do 'without pay'. From this perspective, a universal basic income helps to maintain systems that respect women's human rights and freedoms (Schulz, 2017), such as the freedom to have children and care for them without falling into poverty. On the other hand, a universal basic income could be seen as 'hush money' for the oppression of women (Katada, 2012: 2). One argument against a universal basic income centres on the *reinforcement of gender roles* in society. While a universal basic income might make it easier for women to gain access to the public sphere and for men to access the private sphere, it could also do the opposite, strengthening the gender division of labour (O'Brien, 2017). In other words, a basic income might serve to 'entrench the gendered division of unpaid labour, encouraging those with home-care responsibilities to further withdraw from the labour market' (Higgs, 2018). There is fear among some feminists that a universal basic income could provide a stronger incentive for women to 'undertake unpaid household work and also a greater incentive for men to free ride' (O'Brien, 2017: 102). Free-riding occurs when benefits enjoyed by both partners in a household are produced by only one of them (Van Parijs, 1995). This situation usually benefits men, who reap the advantages of co-habiting with women who are more than often expected to take care of domestic responsibilities in the home. While Van Parijs (1995) remarks that some women would probably use their basic income to 'lighten the double shift' during certain periods of their lives, Pateman (2004: 100) asks whether 'working for a husband at home is the right path either?' suggesting that a basic income could disadvantage rather than advantage women's position and gendered roles. Feminists, for many years, have pointed out that housewives are working (unpaid) by undertaking the necessary responsibilities which housework involves (Oakley, 2019). A basic income might compensate women for the household duties they carry out, but it could also encourage women to work in the home, re-asserting the sexual division of labour.

The debate about universal basic income has been criticized for 'being largely gender blind' (Katada, 2012: 1), as it is often assumed that it will affect men and women in the same, if not identical, ways. It has also been assumed that 'women and their dependents have a lot to gain from such a change' (Schulz, 2017: 91) when actually a universal basic income could have several adverse impacts on women's lives. First, as a stand-alone policy, a basic income is 'unlikely to encourage a fairer distribution of care work' (Higgs, 2018: 3) and will do nothing to discourage women from doing the overwhelming majority of care and domestic work within the home. Second, while a universal basic income compensates women who are more likely than men to work within part-time employment, it also could discourage women from entering the world of work. For example, in Sweden, a subsidy to support parents caring for their own child at home faced strong opposition, because it was seen as a trap for women, preventing them from getting out into the world of work (Higgs, 2018). In other words, a universal basic income could do little to change existing gendered relations between men and women. If it provides an incentive for women to return to the home, more and more women are likely to work part-time, than men. A universal basic income may also do little to change the gender pay gap either, with women, in all sectors of work, earning less than men. In these ways, a universal basic income could exacerbate gender inequalities.

Pateman (2004: 99) says that the private and public sexual division of labour 'continues to be structured so that men monopolize full-time, higher paying, and more prestigious paid employment, and wives do a disproportionate share of unpaid work in the home'. A policy that attempts to mitigate the under-recognized labour in the home through financial re-numeration can have the unintended consequence of discouraging women from access and opportunities in the public sphere (world of work). Following on from these points, Fitzpatrick (1999) argues that a universal basic income does not consider the existing inequality between men and women in the private and public sphere, therefore its equalizing character might actually work to entrench the sexual division of labour and fortify the existing labour market segregation.

From a feminist point of view, Fitzpatrick (1999) identifies three major objections against a universal basic income. Firstly, although a universal basic income embodies a strong element of human rights and the equalizing of men and women in the social care domain, many supporters of basic income confuse the terms de-commodification and de-familiarization. The former refers to freedom from the market; this means ceasing to apply market value to utilities, therefore utilities becoming an entitlement instead of a commodity. With the implementation of a universal basic income this will mean individuals' freedom from the market. In the case of women, while most women are de-commodified they are not de-familiarized, namely freed from household dependencies. Many advocates of universal basic income assume that it would provide freedom which men and women will share equally. However, as Fitzpatrick (1999) argues, they do not consider the familiarization of women in the household and that due to the patriarchal assumptions and values that are ingrained in our society, a universal basic income can in fact worsen the situation for many women and entrench the sexual division of labour. A universal basic income could enable men to greatly enjoy the de-commodification that such a policy can bring (by taking part-time work to pursue their interests and hobbies) while women will continue to care for the household. And although it will bring value to care work, a universal basic income does not assure an equal distribution of it, so a basic income is by no means an ideal form of policy.

Secondly, a universal basic income could also lead to the reinforcement of labour market segregation. While it will allow individuals to choose between paid or unpaid work and allow those in low-wage and part-time jobs choice to disengage from the labour market, most of the individuals with insecure and low-paid jobs are women, therefore the withdrawal from the labour market will lead to a gendered bias detrimental to women. Because women's work is economically worth less in the labour market than men, it is predominantly women who will leave the labour market, opting to not work. For many families, there is less financial risk for the woman to return to the home, and the man to remain as the main 'breadwinner'. In most societies around the world, current norms and values still attach the household and care duties to women, rather than men. If women have the opportunity to exit the labour market without affecting their income, then they would return to household duties, knowing they have a stable income to rely on. Universal basic income is based on the principle of real freedom, however the choice of women leaving the labour force cannot be seen as a genuine wish to not work but a necessity given the circumstances. At worst, a universal basic income could remove women from the world of work, becoming a minimum income for men but a maximum income for women.

Migration, citizenship and the tightening of national borders

A universal basic income can only be achievable and politically feasible if it gets public support. But citizens tend to support redistributive systems which look after 'their own people' to 'whom they owe solidarity', not 'strangers' with whom they have no acquaintance (Van Parijs and Vanderborghts, 2017: 242). Ongoing immigration tends to make populations 'more heterogeneous in racial, religious, and linguistic terms, and this ethnic heterogeneity tends to weaken the political sustainability of a generous redistributive system' (Van Parijs and Vanderborghts, 2017: 242). In order to maintain political support as well as economic sustainability, a highly restrictive border regime is needed to create public support for universal basic income, because a genuine redistribution system requires firm limits on hospitality (Van Parijs and Vanderborghts, 2017). The downside however, is that, apart from 'tightening the borders' (Howard, 2006), the experiences of being 'stranger' or 'outsider' are heightened, as being an immigrant becomes further stigmatized. This can be divisive to society, particularly at a time when right-wing populism has emerged across Europe. Right-wing populism describes groups, politicians and political parties associated with neonationalism, protectionism and anti-immigration policies and practices. Such discourses also appear in the US, where Donald Trump became elected as the man 'to make America great again', as his slogan read. One of the key ways was to restrict immigration, such as his supposed plan of 'building a wall' between Mexico and the US, and focusing on looking after one's own citizens. Similar Trumpian messages of 'Italians first' are sweeping across Italy, particularly with the League Party, whose anti-immigrant policies are tapping into the uncertainties and anxieties of the Italian nation. While universal basic income is intended to provide security and 'look after' its citizens, it can also, by default, *fuel hostility* towards migrants or refugees, who people will begrudge receiving such a generous 'hand-out' from the state. Standing disagrees, arguing that a universal basic income will provide stability, neutralizing and preventing far-right populism and neofascist views:

> A major reason for the growing support for far-right populism, or neo-fascism, is the combination of chronic insecurity and precarity.

A revealing survey in France and Germany found that people had turned to the far-right because they felt devalued as citizens in the economy. The Atavists in the precariat feel they have lost the Past and want it back; they will only resist the lure of populism and xenophobia if offered a secure Present and Future.

(Standing, 2019: 24)

Contrary to arguments that a universal basic income could establish more closely-knit communities resistant to 'intruders' from the outside, fuelling anti-immigrant tendencies, Standing (2019) argues that a universal basic income will offer the security needed to deter people from far-right appeal. Standing (2019: 24) says that 'it is not too fanciful to suggest that a basic income system, by lessening insecurity, precarity, debt and inequality would arrest the drift to populism'.

In an era where xenophobia is rife across Europe and the rest of the globe, we need to understand how 'the progressive majority in advanced democracies can stop people hurtling towards racist, nationalist and misogynist solutions (Mason, 2019: 193). But is universal basic income really the answer? There is evidence to suggest that robust and effective welfare states can attract migrants and generate animosity towards both immigration and the welfare policies themselves. For example, Nordic Europe has become the destination for thousands of migrants and refugees (OECD, 2014), where people are drawn by the promise of social and political inclusion. Universalist societies like Norway, Iceland, Finland, Sweden and Denmark have some of the most 'robust welfare states in the world', historically providing basic living standards to all residents (Ponce, 2018: 1). People will often migrate 'to destinations where co-ethnics have become full-fledged citizens' (Ponce, 2018: 1). However, as a consequence, these parts of Europe have become exposed to migration-led demographic and social changes which have fuelled tensions around universalism and comprehensive welfare policies (Ponce, 2018).

One problem with attempting to implement universal basic income within Europe, is avoiding what has become known as 'the welfare magnet effect' (Ponce, 2018: 1) or 'welfare tourism', where migrants, attracted to the welfare benefits, arrive for new prosperity. The knock-on effect is that countries tighten their borders (Howard, 2006), or make changes in immigration policies or conditions attached to implementing the universal basic income. In European countries with generous welfare policies, 'welfare migration' might pose a problem (Howard, 2006), especially if people arrive in one destination in considerably large numbers. Restricting a universal basic income to 'citizens only' might be seen as one solution to these problems (Howard, 2006), but how you define a 'citizen' then becomes an issue. Should migrant workers or refugees be classified as 'non-citizens'? And should they be refused a universal basic income even though they are residing in the same society? This exclusionary approach is unfair and can result in the exploitation of migrant workers, who may be far more likely to live in poverty, in a society which excludes them a basic means of living.

It is possible that universal basic income could inadvertently 'toughen up' immigration legislation to counteract potential 'welfare migration' (as described earlier). Alternatively, it is possible that a society with universal basic income produces a stratum (level, rank or class) of citizens and non-citizens, with non-citizens devoid of a universal basic income. Historically, having citizenship represents a full spectrum of civil, political, and social rights associated with equal membership in a community. Although many countries provide non-citizens with citizenship, only full-fledged citizens enjoy a complete set of rights (Brochman and Seland, 2010; Ponce, 2018). When examining a range of sociological factors, naturalized immigrants (those who gain full citizenship within a country), are considerably more advantaged than non-citizen immigrants (those without fully fledged citizenship). For instance, naturalized immigrants have lower poverty rates and are generally better-off than non-citizen immigrants (Sainsbury, 2012). Gaining citizenship already provides important status capital and symbolic resources, providing incentive to identify with national cultures (Ponce, 2018). While some marginalized groups in society might benefit from a universal basic income (the poor, or the old, for example), migrants without fully-fledged citizenship and without access to a universal basic income, suddenly become the lowest of the low in society. Non-citizen immigrants become a social group catapulted to the bottom levels of society, not only in terms of money and other social factors, but also now in terms of citizenship status – one of the supposed benefits of having a universal basic income.

While many 'researchers argue that the welfare state, regardless of its type, is under serious strain because of immigration' (Sainsbury, 2012), others argue the opposite, that it is the welfare state which puts strain on migrants. Here, it is universal basic income which could jeopardize the situation for migrants. Overall, the question on the effects of migration is controversial. Any policy implementation will have an effect on people, including what they do and how they will think. A universal basic income will affect people's perceptions on migration, especially if our sense of citizenship and national identity becomes magnified by its implementation. But a universal basic income will also affect 'outsiders' perceptions of a country and migrants might be attracted by the 'welfare magnet' (Ponce, 2018), creating considerable demographic changes across those countries and continents in question. While immigration can have a positive impact in many respects, it can also have adverse effects in some communities, especially if it is perceived within a context where 'being a citizen' carries substantial financial benefits.

Summary

This chapter examined some of the 'against arguments' for universal basic income. It looked at the problems of cost and affordability, 'welfare dependency' and reliance on the welfare state. We saw that there are varied propositions put forward on how to fund a universal basic income, usually through one form of tax or another. But we also saw that any levy will have an adverse impact on people. For example, driving out wealthy tax payers is not an economically wise move given that a universal basic income requires the rich and wealthy for such an expensive policy to be implemented. Indeed, a universal basic income would be one of the most costly welfare reforms of the modern age.

This chapter turned to a range of alternatives to a universal basic income, such as endowment or stake-holding policies (see Ackerman and Alstott, 1999) and Charles Murray's (2006) plan for an 'annual cash grant'. Within these discussions, we showed that there are neoliberal cases made for a basic income (Bowman, 2013) and raised the prospect of a basic income designed and implemented under a right-wing state. We also questioned the adverse effects a universal basic income might have on women, particularly in relation to the 'sexual division of labour', showing how a universal basic income might encourage women to remain within the realm of the home and domestic sphere. We also looked at the effects a universal basic income might have on migration, migrant workers and perceptions of citizenship and rights to a universal basic income – all of which could be undesirable, especially given the current anti-immigrant sentiments expressed across Europe, the US and many other parts of the globe.

References

Ackerman, B. and Alstott, A. (1999) *The Stakeholder Society*. New Haven, CT: Yale University Press.

Altman, S.Falk, A.Jäger, S. and Zimmerman, F. (2017) 'Learning about job search: A field experiment with job seekers in Germany'. Retrieved from https://papers.ssrn.com/sol3/papers.cfm?abstract_id=2613354

Atkinson, A. (1996) 'The case for a participation income'. *The Political Quarterly*, 67(1), pp.67–70.

Barry, B. (2001) 'UBI and the work ethic'. In: P. Van Parijs, ed. *What's Wrong With a Free Lunch?* Boston, MA: Beacon Press.

Birnbaum, S. (2004) 'Real libertarianism, structural injustice and the democratic ideal'. Paper presented at The Right to a Basic Income: Egalitarian Democracy, BIEN's 10th Congress, Barcelona.

Bowman, S. (2013) 'The ideal welfare system is a basic income'. Retrieved from www.adamsmith.org/blog/welfare-pensions/the-ideal-welfare-system-is-a-basic-income

Brochmann, G. and Seland, I. (2010) 'Citizenship policies and ideas of nationhood in Scandinavia'. *Citizenship Studies* 14(4): 429–443.

Fitzpatrick, T. (1999) *Freedom and Security: An Introduction to the Basic Income Debate*. London: Macmillan.

Friedman, M. (1962) *Capitalism and Freedom*. Chicago, IL: University of Chicago Press.

Goldin, I. (2018) 'Five reasons why a basic income is a bad idea'. *Financial Times*, 11 February. Retrieved from www.ft.com/content/100137b4-0cdf-11e8-bacb-2958fde95e5e

Gheaus, A. (2008) 'Basic income, gender justice and the costs of gender-symmetrical lifestyles'. *Basic Income Studies*, 3(3).

Guardian (2019) 'Labour would trial universal basic income if elected, John McDonnell says'. *The Guardian*, 12 May. Retrieved from www.theguardian.

com/society/2019/may/12/labour-would-trial-universal-basic-incom
e-if-elected-john-mcdonnell-says

Henderson, D. (2015) 'A philosophical economist's case against a government-guaranteed basic income'. *The Independent Review*, 19(4), pp. 489–502.

Higgs, R. (2018) 'Is basic income a solution to persistent inequalities faced by women?' Retrieved from http://theconversation.com/is-a-basic-incom
e-the-solution-to-persistent-inequalities-faced-by-women-92939

Howard, M. (2006) 'Basic income and migration policy: A moral dilemma?'. *Basic Income Studies*, 1(1).

Katada, K. (2012) 'Basic income and feminism: in terms of "the gender division of labour"'. Retrieved from https://basicincome.org/bien/pdf/munich2012/katada.pdf

Katz, M. B. (2013) *The Undeserving Poor*. Oxford: Oxford University Press.

Levine, A. (1995) 'Fairness to idleness: Is there a right not to work?'. *Economics and Philosophy*, 11(2), pp. 255–274.

Martinelli, L. (2017) *Assessing the Case for a Universal Basic Income in the UK*. Bath: University of Bath.

Mason, P. (2019) *Clear Bright Future: Radical Defence of Being Human*. London: Penguin.

Murray, C. (1984) *Losing Ground: American Social Policy 1950–1980*. New York: Basic Books.

Murray, C. (2006) *In Our Hands: A Plan to Replace the Welfare State*. Washington, DC: The AEI Press.

Oakley, A. (2019) *The Sociology of Housework*. Bristol: Polity Press.

O'Brien, P. (2017) *Universal Basic Income: Pennies from Heaven*. Stroud: The History Press.

O'Hagan, E. M. (2017) 'Love the idea of a universal basic income? Be careful what you wish for'. *The Guardian*, 23 June.

OECD. 2014. *International Migration Outlook 2014*. Paris: Organisation for Economic Co-operation and Development.

Orloff, A. (2013) 'Why basic income does not promote gender equality'. In: K. Widerquist, J. Noguera, Y. Vanderborght and J. De Wispelaere, eds. *Basic Income: An Anthology of Contemporary Research*. Oxford: John Wiley & Sons, pp. 149–153.

Parncutt, R. (2012) 'Universal basic income and flat income tax: Tax justice, incentive, economic democracy'. Paper at 14th BIEN Conference, Munich, Germany, 14–16 September. Retrieved from https://basicincome.org/bien/pdf/munich2012/parncutt.pdf

Pasma, C. (2010) 'Working through the work disincentive'. *Basic Income Studies*, 5(2).

Pateman, C. (2004) 'Democratizing citizenship: Some advantages of a basic income'. *Politics and Society*, 32(1), pp. 89–105.

Phelps, E. (2001) 'Subsidize wages'. In: P. Van Parijs, ed. *What's Wrong With a Free Lunch? Boston: Beacon Press.* Boston, MA: Beacon Press.

Ponce, A. (2018) 'Is welfare a magnet for migration? Examining universal welfare institutions and migration flows'. *Social Forces Journal*, November.

Sainsbury, D. (2012) *Welfare States and Immigrant Rights: The Politics of Inclusion and Exclusion.* Oxford: Oxford University Press.

Schulz, P. (2017) 'Universal basic income in a feminist perspective and gender analysis'. *Global Social Policy*, 17(1), pp. 89–92.

Standing, G. (2019) *Basic Income as Common Dividends: Piloting a Transformative Policy.* London: Progressive Economy Forum.

Stevens, M. (2019) 'Elizabeth Warren on a wealth tax'. *The New York Times*, 30 July. Retrieved from www.nytimes.com/2019/07/30/us/politics/elizabeth-warren-wealth-tax.html

Van Donselaar, G. (2009) *The Right to Exploit: Parasitism, Scarcity, Basic Income.* Oxford: Oxford University Press.

Van Parijs, P. (1995) *Freedom for All.* Oxford: Oxford University Press.

Van Parijs, P. and Vanderborght, Y. (2017) *Basic Income: A Radical Proposal for a Free Society and a Sane Economy.* Cambridge, MA: Harvard University Press.

White, S. (1997) 'Liberal equality, exploitation, and the case for an unconditional basic income'. *Political Studies*, 45(2), pp. 312–326.

Zwolinski, M. (2010) 'Review: *The Right to Exploit: Parasitivism, Scarcity, Basic Income*, Gijs Van Donselaar [Review]'. Retrieved from https://digital.sandiego.edu/cgi/viewcontent.cgi?article=1067&context=philosophy_facpub

8

REFLECTIONS ON UNIVERSAL BASIC INCOME

Introduction

This textbook has provided an introduction to universal basic income. It began by outlining what some believe to be a radical or crazy idea – a no-strings-attached regular income from the state – guaranteed to every citizen regardless of their personal circumstances. A universal basic income has been called various things: 'citizen's income'; 'citizen's wage'; 'universal grant'; 'universal dividend', and 'guaranteed universal subsidy' (see Chapter 1) and in various pilots and experiments around the world, variations of a 'universal basic income' have gone by a variety of different names: Unconditional Cash Transfers (Madhya Pradesh, India); Basic Income Grants (Namibia); Permanent Fund Dividend (Alaska, US) Cash Subsidy Scheme (Iran). Many of these examples (described in Chapter 4) cannot, strictly speaking, be classified as a universal basic income. Many were not designed as a universal basic income and those which were, often fall short of a 'universal basic income' by the very fact that they are mere experiments or pilots which are either trialled for only a short length of time, and/or are essentially non-universal. Take for instance, Finland's *perustulokeilu* ('basic income' experiment) which only targeted those out of work. Its narrow focus on unemployed people arguably fails to understand the *genuine effects* a 'universal' basic income has on a given society. To date, there has not been a fully, or properly, implemented universal basic income anywhere in the world, although we believe that the unconditional cash transfers in Madhya Pradesh, India, comes closest to one (given the size and scope of the 'trials').

Some ask why no country around the world has never fully implemented a universal basic income? Critics use this as justification for saying a universal basic income is inadequate – because if it were so good, some country, somewhere, would have implemented it successfully. But that's a poor argument, as we cannot say that a new policy or welfare implementation will fail, just because it has not been carried out before. Many in Britain thought that the proposal to create a free healthcare service, pushed forward by the post-war British health minister Aneurin ('Nye') Bevan, was a crazy and too radical of an idea. But the National Health Service (NHS) has been considered, by most, to be a huge success – even some seventy years later. Likewise, the idea that profits from Alaskan oil revenues would be shared out with every Alaskan citizen, seemed radical and incomprehensible by many, but it was made possible and has stood the test of time. We believe that most current welfare systems, like those developed in Britain, the US and most European countries are unfit for purpose and in drastic need of change. Problems of means testing; stigmatization; lack of universality; the unemployment trap, and failure to deal with profound levels of poverty make traditional forms of welfare unsuitable for the modern era.

The idea of a universal basic income may have been around for a long time, as we pointed out in the introductory chapter, but the appetite for a universal basic income right now has never been stronger. Countries around the world are experimenting and piloting with forms of universal basic income. Some of them stop midway through the experiment, or call off the idea altogether, but this is often more to do with changes in political leadership than necessarily the failure of the project itself. Furthermore, as one basic income pilot or experiment stops in one country or place, another one or two start up elsewhere. In the UK for example, universal basic income is a topic of discussion for both the political right and left, although approaches may vary quite considerably – hence why some advocates, such as Standing (2019), say a basic income should be managed by an independent authority, so it is not changed every time a new political party takes leadership. Of course debates on whether a universal basic income will work wholly depend upon the circumstances in which it is implemented. We do not believe that there is an easy answer to whether or not a universal basic income will prove successful or not, because much depends on who will implement it, how it is implemented and also how generous or well managed it will be. With every basic income proposal put forward, 'it is important to look at the details of the proposal – not just at the level of the basic income and how obligation-free it is, but also at what it is meant to replace and how it is supposed to be financed' (Van Parijs and Vanderborght, 2017: 196). How effective a basic income is much depends on *all* of these factors.

The rest of this chapter provides further reflections on a universal basic income. The aim is to consider basic income from a number of standpoints we have laid out throughout the course of this textbook. This includes reflecting on universal basic income from some of the key underlying principles we laid out in the theory chapter: inequality, freedom and social justice. But it also means reflecting on universal basic income from the themes we have focussed on too, such as precariousness, poverty and social inequality; health and wellbeing, and the ecological impact. Not least, we must reflect on universal basic income by revisiting some of the against arguments we laid out in Chapter 7, by looking at the impact on women's lives, examining how it might affect national identity, citizenship and migration and evaluating universal basic income against some of the alternatives. Finally, the overall aim of this textbook has been to facilitate the learning of students and readers of basic income, with the key ideas necessary to make sense of the topic and with the tools with which to navigate around the various issues and examples. We hope that this chapter offers a framework with which you can reflect upon your own understanding of universal basic income, or use it as a tool for revision, so that you can better develop your own thoughts and arguments around universal basic income.

Inequality, freedom and social justice

Throughout this text, we have shown that a universal basic income has gathered momentum all over the world, with countries continually discussing and trialling it. With every trial or experiment comes a political and philosophical discussion about the underlying principles of universal basic income. In Chapter 2, we laid out inequality, freedom and social justice as some of these fundamental principles, by discussing several theorists whose ideas strongly resonate with those advocating for a universal basic income. For example, a key theory underpinning some of the key values of universal basic income is John Rawls's (1999) *A Theory of Justice* (first published 1971). Rawls's book provides a framework around the notion of social justice, detailing how society and its institutions should put social justice at the heart of what they do, as a way which can counteract social inequalities. Rawls's (1999) theory laid out three principles, ordered hierarchically, including the liberty principle (fundamental freedoms such as the right to vote and the freedom of expression), the principle of fair equality of opportunity (requiring people to have equal access to all social positions) and the difference principle (requiring that the worst social position in society should be as high as possible). It is this last principle, in particular, which we said really supported the idea of a universal basic income (see Chapter 2). These Rawlsian principles are not simply about guaranteeing a minimum level of consumption, but also relate to the idea of wealth, which fits with the ideals of a universal basic income. Rawls himself did not push for a universal basic income, but did suggest a negative income tax, a similar kind of redistributive system of income. He thought there was great value in the self-worth such an income can give, especially in contrast to the stigmatized and humiliating 'benefits' that many countries provide within existing welfare regimes. In the opening chapter, we described the situation experienced by a British man, narrated in the film *I, Daniel Blake*. Redundant and out of work, the middle-aged man was sent pillar to post, forced to attend administrative meetings and to job hunt for any work at all, and in many ways made to feel like a criminal. Stories like this are all too typical and make the Rawlsian argument to social justice all the more convincing.

The idea of freedom and liberty were discussed in relation to Van Parijs and Vanderborght's (2017) notion of 'real freedom for all', laid out in *Basic Income: A Radical Proposal for a Free Society and Sane Economy*. In this work, the idea that a capitalist system provides freedom can become problematic, because we readily misunderstand what 'real freedom' actually involves. An individual living in New York or Berlin might have the 'choice' and 'freedom' to buy property. But if property prices are sky high then the freedom and choice become limited or taken away. Van Parijs and Vanderborght's (2017) showed us that there are different types of freedom which we must understand when thinking about welfare policies. Van Parijs said that libertarians created a concept of the State based on the creation of rights and a system that can protect and reinforce these rights, but failed to recognize the *involvement and engagement* in these rights. A person's purchasing power, in terms of real freedom, for example, is not only a matter of having the right to do what one might want to do, but also a matter of having the means or ability to be able to do it (see Van Parijs, 1997). A universal basic income has the potential to provide a 'real-freedom-for-all'.

For some critics of a universal basic income, an individual's freedom is thwarted by the imposition of a potential new tax, which inflicts itself upon people, by reducing their freedom to live the lives they choose. In Hayek's *Constitution of Liberty* (first published in 1960), the notion of freedom or liberty (which he uses interchangeably) depends upon the meaning of the concept of coercion. For Hayek, coercion is 'control of the environment or circumstances of a person by another that, in order to avoid greater evil, he is forced to act not according to a coherent plan of his own but to serve the ends of another' (Hayek, 2006: 19). This serving the ends of another, which is valued by many advocates of universal basic income, can also be seen as an infringement of rights and freedom of an individual. British prime minister Margaret Thatcher's phrase that 'there's no such thing as society, only individuals' was a direct influence of Hayek's philosophy. She was emphasizing the freedom of the individual to make their own choices on how to live their lives. But the size and scope of a universal basic income is seen by some as a mammoth extension of the welfare (and 'nanny') state – a direct interference to the individual's life. When a third of your earnings (depending which country you live in) are taxed and redistributed to others, the capacity for you (now with less income) to live how you want can become restrained. So there are different ways of thinking about 'freedom'.

Precariousness, poverty and social inequality

In Chapter 3, we examined universal basic income in relation to the notion of 'the precariat' (Standing, 2015). We saw that precarious work was rife across the globe, with people from all kinds of sectors of work experiencing insecure, non-standard work, with unprotected and poor quality working conditions. Following Standing (2019: 19), the precariat's position is exacerbated by the fact that they are *supplicants* – people who have to 'rely on asking people for favours, for permission, for help, which if not granted threaten their ability to function'. Instead of lacking dignity and depending on the goodwill of others, people can become empowered through a universal basic income, by having the means to live as ordinary citizens. 'Millions of people are living bits-and-pieces lives' (Standing, 2019: 19), because they do not have the means to provide themselves and their families with a basic level of social and economic security. With globalization and labour supply driven by unpredictable market forces, and the predicted growth of automated technologies, the precariat cannot rely on the labour market to provide the necessary employment opportunities to escape poverty. Precarious workers who are subject to insecure, unprotected and poorly paid working conditions can be supported by a basic income which can supplement their earnings, and/or provide a safety net for periods in which work, or working hours, are scarce. Universal basic income cannot eradicate all poverty or resolve all social inequalities, but it can compensate for some of the financial problems created by a neoliberal economy.

A universal basic income becomes attractive because it offers, at least theoretically speaking, a stable and secure safety net for individuals to live their lives. Marxist writer Gorz (1999) added that notions of what 'work' is needs to be reinterpreted to encompass the human activities people are involved with in day-to-day life – such as raising children; caring for elderly relatives, and contributing to the local community and society in a plethora of ways. The Victorian notion of the 'work ethic' still saturates our common sense thinking of 'work'. Those who are not working are deemed idle because capitalism has conditioned us to believe that paid employment is a human necessity and has value. As a consequence, non-paid employment is valueless, or at least insignificant in comparison. Of course, Gorz (1999) argued that paid employment need not be a necessity at all. For example, one way some countries have resourced welfare payments is through the use of natural resources. Although neither Iran's Nationwide Cash Subsidy Scheme, nor Alaska's Permanent Fund Dividend are, technically speaking, 'universal basic income', both provide cash payments to citizens by distributing income received from oil revenues. This use of natural resources is one way of achieving an egalitarian society in which everyone benefits equally from the society in which they live.

Health and wellbeing

In Chapter 4, we outlined a broad range of examples, where basic income trials and experiments had been carried out. Examples showed that regular cash payments helped people to eradicate debts; develop new skills for work, and invest in small businesses. But examples also showed us that investing in a person's wellbeing, such as providing basic food, water and/or improving home sanitation, could be equally as productive for families. Communities cannot prosper if hindered by poor health or inadequate levels of sanitation. Throughout this text, we have shown how a universal basic income can provide a means of improving the health and wellbeing of individuals and whole communities. Take for example, Ontario's Guaranteed Minimum Income, where resources improved diets, access to medical professionals and a means to purchase better medicines and medical equipment (see Chapter 4). A universal basic income can also minimize the chances of having poor mental health and having stress related illnesses such as 'heart disease, diabetes, autoimmune diseases, upper respiratory infections and poorer wound healing' (Standing, 2019: 18).

In Finland's *perustulokeilu* (basic income experiment), we saw that people were happier and less stressed with the arrival of a basic income, regardless of whether or not it improved their ability to find employment. In Namibia's Basic Income Grant (BIG), recipients reported better health and nutrition, and a reduction of those below the food poverty line. In Ethiopia's USAID two-year basic income scheme, recipients health was a major factor, since the improvement of basic nutrition meant that children were more likely to attend school and adults were more likely to be able to work, with less chance of falling ill (again, see Chapter 4). The accumulative effects of these health and wellbeing advantages are clear to see. A regular income means better nutrition, better health, more able family members and a better chance of living in a healthy community. In countries where there are out-breaks of difficult to control diseases, the health of whole communities can benefit from the introduction of a universal basic income, because you are far less likely to fall ill if those around you are healthy.

Put simply, a universal basic income can improve both the physical health and mental wellbeing of a person, which also has knock-on effects for the mental health and wellbeing of her or his family. Stand-ing (2019: 17) says there is a 'pandemic of stress' which is causing a 'morbidity crisis' involving 'more physical and mental ill-health' (Standing, 2019: 17). Income insecurity causes stress and leads to what Standing (2019: 18) describes as a reduction or narrowing of 'mental bandwidth', causing people to focus on short-term choices and goals, rather than strategically thinking about long-term solutions. When people are deprived and struggling to make ends meet, it is their mental health which also suffers, exacerbating what is already a desperate situation. Stress is 'compounded by money worries' (Standing, 2019: 18), and in countries like Britain, where there is much anxiety about fulfilling conditions for means-tested benefits, the mental capacity to cope only becomes worse. In all, a universal basic income can reduce health-related illness, including the problems associated with high levels of stress.

The impact on women

In Chapter 5, we outlined several arguments concerning the work of women and universal basic income, laying out a feminist economics perspective to generally explore whether or not women would be better-off or worse-off from the introduction of a universal basic income. Drawing on various feminist perspectives, the chapter exam-ined the extent to which a universal basic income could increase women's independence and economic power. Universal basic income showed it could be empowering for women in many ways, by lifting them out of poverty, for example, by providing an additional source of income which might compensate them for raising children. However, while a universal basic income might be said to emancipate women, by giving them more economic freedom, for instance, we also saw that 'freedom' was a complex issue and that a universal basic income could also encourage traditional forms of family life – entrenching women inside the home and discouraging them from active participation in the world of work. Indeed, women may continue to carry the domestic burden of unpaid care work and so long-term prospects could, potentially be, rather dismal with an introduction of universal basic income.

Professor Susan Himmelweit, from the Progressive Economy Forum and Women's Budget Group (UK), believes that there could be a number of great benefits to a universal basic income (such as getting rid of means testing) but she also raised concerns that a universal basic income could be detrimental to the lives of women.[1] Himmelweit's concern is that we exercise freedom by making choices in a world full of gendered norms, thus we all know that it will be predominantly women, not men, who are going to be at home doing the care. Himmelweit believes that for a universal basic income to work, the care system needs to be looked at as well, and that could be very expensive. These concerns are just one of many potential problems with the introduction of a universal basic income – any implementation must seriously take into consideration the impact on women and the added costs required to 'fix up' other parts of the welfare system.

Proposals 'for' a universal basic income tend to brandish women as an homogeneous group, with failure to map out, or intellectualize, how a universal basic income might differently affect the lives of women from varied social groups and positions. Using the notion of intersectionality, our chapter on 'the work of women' (again, see Chapter 5) examined the diverse and varied experiences of women, by looking at gender in relation to ethnicity, age, social class and the different kinds of gendered experiences they are confronted with due to country and circumstance. In all, we showed that the effects of universal basic income can vary depending on the experiences of different social groups of women, in different contexts and within different periods of their lives. We believe that these experiences need to be considered more carefully before introducing a universal basic income.

The ecological impact

In Chapter 6, we asked in what ways a universal basic income might impact on the environment? We outlined arguments, from Green parties, eco-activists and social scientists, that a universal basic income could change the mind-set and practices of people helping us to move beyond a society driven by production, consumption and growth. Society is currently set up in a way that celebrates and rewards individualistic and materialist ways of living even though these are ecologically detrimental to society (Jackson, 2017). This has brought a new era, some called the Anthropocene, where human activity is radically changing the Earth's environment. Shifting the materialist and growth mind-set can be facilitated by a universal basic income, not because it is set up to cripple the economy, but because it promotes values which are crucial to the functioning of a healthy society. Universal basic income can help shape a society where consuming less is possible – hence why it has been supported by green parties all over Europe and the rest of the globe (see Van Parijs and Vanderborght, 2017). Thus universal basic income offers a route towards a 'post-growth' economy – meeting our needs without having to compromise the needs of future generations (Seyfang, 2011).

A universal basic income can provide better recognition of those engaged in child care and promote the values of those who work in the voluntary and community sectors. It can radically transform the dynamics of work so that we shift the focus away from 'status competition' and towards a 'more altruistic society' (Jackson, 2017: 7). We need to value the 'real work' people do which enables our society to function (Gorz, 1999) recognizing that not everybody need be earning an income to contribute to a healthy society. Universal basic income is one way of investing more ethically in society, where people can be more family oriented, enjoy time with relatives and friends, many of whom they will care for and which will benefit their health and well-being. This might have little to do with output or efficiency but everything to do with prosperity and is of course healthier for the environment (Jackson, 2017).

But a universal basic income is not the only way to tackle these environmental problems. Instead of pursuing low consumption lifestyles we can move towards a greener capitalism in which we can generate cleaner economic growth (Seyfang, 2011: 3). There is a whole new raft of environmental markets which are 'big business' and which create economic growth, only in a different way, which is kinder to the planet in which we live. People can still purchase the latest goods, so long as they are renewable, sustainable, and not bad for the environment. For instance, the expansion of the vintage clothes market or the use of sea plastics to produce swim wear for children, are examples of how forms of consumerism can exist without being detrimental to the environment. The windfarm technologies and solar panel systems which developed, bought, sold and rented are all big business. So there are other ways in which society can change, regardless of whether or not a universal basic income is in place. We believe that a universal basic income could play a part in helping the environment, but we are aware that there are other ways too.

National identity, citizenship and migration

In a world where there has been 'an erosion of social solidarity linked to excessive individualism and competition' (Standing, 2019: 6), a universal basic income would provide a sense of belonging, linked to citizenship and sense of national pride. A universal basic income would 'strengthen social solidarity' because it would be 'an expression that we are all part of a national community sharing the benefits of the national public wealth created over our collective history' (Standing, 2019: 6). A universal basic income might be paid to individuals, but it is not individualistic, in the sense that it is universal and equal 'in stark contrast to means-tested social assistance or tax credits' (Standing, 2019: 6). A universal basic income instils a sense of identity and provides 'social glue', bringing together the community, providing a sense of pride and self-worth.

But wherever there are strong community ties and feelings of belonging to an inside group, there is also usually a strong sense of who is *not* with the in-group, 'the outsiders'. Citizens often will support redistributive systems which look after those with whom they share solidarity (Van Parijs and Vanderborghts, 2017), not strangers or outsiders. We showed that a universal basic income could prompt strict border controls (see Chapter 7), with stricter forms of immigration, to provide 'firm limits on hospitality' (Van Parijs and Vanderborghts, 2017: 242). Some said that this would be a response to 'welfare tourism' or the 'welfare magnet effect' (Ponce, 2018: 1), where families sensibly head towards countries offering the most secure welfare provisions. Along with this can come resentment and a backlash on migrant workers and families, in which xenophobia and racist beliefs are fuelled by perceptions of outsiders who come to 'scrounge' off the hard work or wealth of others.

There are fears that strengthening the sense of social solidarity will feed into far-right populism, having resonance with US President Trump's slogan of 'America first', where tensions towards migrants have become exacerbated by notions of insider and outsider. However, Standing (2019) believes that a universal basic income can help to stamp out aggressive nationalism and anti-immigration posturing. Standing (2019) argues that the growing support of right-wing populism is brought about by chronic insecurity and precarity. By reducing debt and inequality, recipients of a universal basic income would be less attracted to political parties of the far right. Blaming immigrants and other marginalized groups for our social problems has long been a narrative played out by politicians and the media (McDonough, 2017). Much of this 'blame' has been apportioned to 'outsiders' to cover-up the enormous disparities in wealth, so that everyday citizens blame immigrants and other vulnerable groups, instead of challenging the powerful elite. Universal basic income offers a way of redressing some of these wealth inequalities.

Alternatives to a universal basic income

In Chapter 7, we outlined a number of alternatives to a universal basic income, along with some discussion of different variations of the policy. One alternative was the 'stakeholder idea', which involved giving a large sum, like US$80,000, to every citizen when they turn twenty-one years old (Ackerman and Alstott, 1999: 8). Rather than thinking about a 'minimum provision' as a basic income does, the aim of the 'stakeholder idea' is to maximize opportunity and success. The 'stakeholder idea', or idea of giving a large endowment to adults at the start of adult life, is very appealing. Arguably, it can give adults a chance to get on the property ladder, invest in education, training or skills, or just provide enough income to set up a family life (marriage, car and kids). This idea may think of the family in a more conservative way, but then so does a universal basic income, with its obvious (though unintended) influence of attracting women towards domestic life within the home.

So there are pros and cons to a stakeholder approach, as there are pros and cons to a universal basic income.

Charles Murray (2006) also proposed a plan to see every citizen over the age of twenty-one (in the US) receive a cash grant. But with his idea, recipients would receive US$10,000 per year, allowed to spend the fund however they wish. Again there are similarities with a universal basic income, as people get 'free cash' for virtue of being a citizen, regardless of whether they work or not. Murray's (2006) plan could arguably offer more flexibility and 'freedom' because like Ackerman and Alstott's (1999) 'Stakeholder' idea, it provides the annual US $10,000 up front, rather than processing payments weekly or monthly. Getting large lump sums can be hugely advantageous. Even in studies of basic income trials and experiments, recipients have reported pooling their money together in order to carryout significant changes in their lives (Devala et al., 2015). This could involve fixing a roof; sending a family member to school or university; or purchasing transport (a bicycle, motorcycle or car) to enable family members to find better work. Giving people large amounts of cash up front can be life-changing and can enable people to invest in their lives without needing to pool together resources or to save up money. Endowment or stakeholder funds, or whatever they may be called, can provide alternative options to a universal basic income. We believe that these are viable alternatives to a universal basic income which should not be dismissed.

Summary

This chapter has reflected on a number of recurring themes raised throughout this text, inequality, freedom and social justice; precariousness, poverty and social inequality; health and wellbeing; the impact on women; the environment; national identity, citizenship and migration, and alternatives to a universal basic income. In each of these sections we have reflected on the debates laid out in previous chapters, providing an overall summary that we believe gives a balanced position on the question of universal basic income. These sections offer students and readers of universal basic income an opportunity to think over some of the issues raised throughout this textbook. It has offered a summary of key debates and ideas but with some of our own opinions clearly stated.

Overall, we believe that a universal basic income could fail if it is developed with bad intentions or with the wrong values. For example, using it as a blanket payment to mollify whole communities, pacifying them in desperate times, or replacing existing welfare provision if it can be done 'on the cheap', is clearly not a positive policy to implement. However, if it is served to rejuvenate the lives and aspirations of people – by providing an income which can be used to counteract social injustice and inequality, then it could prove successful. But much depends on the amount provided, the way it is implemented, and how boundaries around who can qualify for a basic income can be enforced – tightening the borders as Van Parijs and Vanderborght's (2017) suggest may happen, will become a political and economic debate in itself.

Thinking about how a universal basic income might impact on the lives of women, and women of different age, social class and ethnicity all needs to be taken into account more seriously. A universal basic income also needs to be implemented with a view to adjusting other welfare systems in society (such as the care system, for instance). But more than anything, we should not pin all our hopes on a universal basic income resolving all of society's problems (poverty; unemployment; crime; global warming) because it can only work successfully if it was implemented as part of a wider policy context where other aspects of the social system change too. We should also remember that it is not the only solution – but that there are alternatives, or variations, which might be worth trialling and implementing too.

Note

1 Professor Himmelweit's comments were made during a question from the floor at a panel discussion around Guy Standing's *Basic Income as Common Dividends* report (Standing, 2019). The entire discussion is available at www.youtube.com/watch?v=8nJRKxIboMU, and Professor Himmelweit's contribution begins at 1:11:50.

References

Ackerman, B. and Alstott, A. (1999) *The Stakeholder Society*. New Haven, CT: Yale University Press.

Devala, S., Jhabvala, R., Mehta, S. K. and Standing, G. (2015) *Basic Income: A Transformative Policy for India*. London: Bloomsbury.

Gorz, A. (1999) *Reclaiming Work: Beyond a Wage Based Society.* Cambridge: Cambridge Policy Press.

Hayek, F. A. (2006) *The Constitution of Liberty.* Abingdon: Routledge.

Jackson, T. (2017) *Prosperity Without Growth: Foundations for the Economy of Tomorrow.* New York: Routledge.

Maniates, M. (2002) 'Individualisation: Plant a tree, buy a bike, save a world?'. In: T. Princen, M. Maniates and K. Konka, eds. *Confronting Consumption.* Cambridge, MA: MIT Press.

McDonough, B. (2017) 'Precarious work and unemployment in Europe'. In: S. Isaacs, ed. *European Social Problems.* Abingdon: Routledge.

Murray, C. (2006) *In Our Hands: A Plan to Replace the Welfare State.* Washington, DC: The AEI Press.

Ponce, A. (2018) 'Is welfare a magnet for migration? Examining universal welfare institutions and migration flows'. *Social Forces Journal*, November.

Rawls, J. (1999) *A Theory of Justice.* Cambridge, MA: Belknap Press.

Seyfang, G. (2011) *The New Economics of Sustainable Consumption.* Basingstoke: Palgrave Macmillan.

Standing, G. (2015) *The Precariat: A New Dangerous Class.* London: Penguin.

Standing, G. (2019) *Basic Income as Common Dividends: Piloting a Transformative Policy.* London: Progressive Economy Forum.

Van Parijs, P. (1997) *Real Freedom for All: What (if anything) Can Justify Capitalism?* Oxford: Clarendon Press.

Van Parijs, P. and Vanderborght, Y. (2017) *Basic Income: A Radical Proposal for a free Society and a Sane Economy.* Cambridge, MA: Harvard University Press.

INDEX